It is easier to deceive people

than to persuade them that

they have been deceived

(Or the story of my divorce

from a Thai woman

Or much ado about nothing)

Contents

Chapter 1 : some ideas

I wonder if anyone from the West has stood up in Thai court and refused to pay bail? I doubt it – all the Western people have tried everything to avoid going to prison in Thailand. After all, you would not call them a hotel or paradise! I have heard of a Westerner paying over £10,000 to stay out of prison. The judges were, to say the least, surprised and my own lawyer was urging me to pay. However, I had packed a bag ready to go to prison and I had informed my wife and her lawyer that I was not going to pay bail the next morning in the court. I don' think anyone believed me. I will let you into a little secret – I was prepared to go as I had looked at the cost and benefits of going to prison in Thailand and decided that it was worth it. I would lose weight and save money!

I decided to write this book because too many people from the West and particularly the British just allow people in Thailand to take all their money and possessions when they divorce. I want to show through my experience that the legal system in Thailand is not corrupt and that the Police in Thailand can be very supportive to Western people in Thailand. The aim of this book is to show that you can keep your investment in Thailand but you have to have a very strong character and be prepared that it will take a long time and you will be attacked in all sorts of ways by your Thai wife and her family. The system in Thailand is very slow as they believe strongly in negotiation so you will spend many hours and days and weeks in meetings with Judges.

You must remember that the Thai wife and her family will make all sorts of allegations about you. They will make false criminal complaints about you. They will lie in statements to the court. They will make all sorts of sexual allegations about you. They will come in a group to try and take assets from you. They will try to intimidate you. They will steal from you. In the end you can win and keep everything you paid for. Even if you do not have the original paperwork and even if you did not obtain a lease contract you can still keep your assets in Thailand.

It is clear that I have won in Thailand as my wife is now trying to claim there was no divorce going on in Thailand and that the divorce should be in the UK. She knows that she has lost in Thailand as the court in Thailand has turned against her and her family. She is now trying to have the divorce in the UK. That has happened because I was not prepared to just give up like too many men my age.

Men of my age have become very weak. They give in. They give in in the UK and Thailand. I hate that because it emboldens women to tell lies and to make false allegations. I have met many men my age in the UK; Thailand and China who have all given up in divorce and ended up with the debts and none of the assets. The men then don't like me as I didn't give in. This highlights there abject failure.

I have a very strong character and I don't care what you say about me – I only care if other people take it seriously. I don't like people lying about me. People can criticise me as long as they have a proper basis for it and it is the truth. I always say to people – if you don't like what I am doing then tell me and I will see if I want to change it. At performance review meetings at work I would also say to my manager I know what my weaknesses are – some I choose to live with, some I try to change.

I can be very stubborn; I can be capricious; I can be a pain in the bum. This allied with a high intelligence can be a potent mix if I am bored or get angry about something. This allied with a tough background means it is very difficult to intimidate me. I have an IQ of between 141 to 145. I only found that out when I was about 40 years old. I used to scared of heights but at 18 I decided it was silly so I forced myself to climb up ladders to the house roof height and now it is not a problem. I used to totally scared of spiders and at about 25 I decided it was silly so I taught myself to handle spiders – very big spiders I still have a problem with them. I have taught myself to repair motorbike engines and to be able to strip down a motorbike engine and put it back together. As I have got older I take more risks – I ride a motorbike faster now that 25 years ago and I take part in sports that are more riskier than 25 years ago. My brother calls me an adrenaline junkie – I am happy with that insult!

Being my age I have seen a lot in the UK. I was lucky because of when I was born. Governments in the UK used to believe in trying to improve the lives of its citizens – I remember during elections in the 70s that all parties would pledge to build thousands of government housing and increase pensions. This does not happen anymore. The British people have been brainwashed in believing that the UK cannot afford to build government housing or pay pensions at a level that people can live on in the UK. So many times after the financial crash 2008 British people would state that we could not afford pensions in the UK. This was while the Bankers were receiving billions in bonuses while the UK

Government owed the shares of those banks and reducing pensions for everyone in the UK. As someone said – the British nationalised the debt of Banks and the bonuses and privatised the profits! The British people are too stupid to realise it!

You can watch many videos made by Western men about how they lost everything in Thailand to their Thai wives. They gave up without a fight and assumed that they could not win. The believed the lies they were told by Thai people and listened to other men who just gave up. I watched a video on the Internet and the man from the UK told how he had bought a farm and then the wife took control of the money in the relationship and she basically made his life intolerable in Thailand. So he just gave up and returned to the UK with just his clothes and no money. Gave up without a fight – too many men my age are the same and I despise them.

I think my Thai wife thought I would be the same. Very insulting. I never give in or allow people to steal things from me. You would think that my wife who had been married to me for 12 years and known me for 14 years would have worked that out. It appears not. Friends of mine and my brother all said that she clearly did not know me as they knew I would react as I did.

I worked in the Metropolitan police for 13 years and the very senior police officers in the Met Police never intimidated me; even I went to courts in the UK I was never intimidated and threats in the UK have never intimidated me. Why did my wife think that the threat of prison in Thailand would intimidate me?

My theory is that my wife was told by people in the UK and Thailand that she could get everything from me on divorce. They didn't realise that I do my research. I was always prepared in the Met Police when it came to negotiations with senior management - I knew the rules; I knew the systems and I knew the part of the law that covered those negotiations.

I always appear to be laid back and too lazy to do the research but I always do.

The one thing I found out was that the law in Thailand is very useful when it comes to divorce. The biggest mistake that my wife made was to be too greedy. As a consequence it is very likely she will be paying me money at the end of the process.

We are in the process and I think based on my experience in the UK it will take another 3 years in the UK. There is at the time of writing still no date for a hearing in the UK to decide if the UK court has jurisdiction in this matter. I started the divorce in Thailand 2 years ago and then suddenly my wife has tried to transfer it to the UK. I think silly because she could have had 50% of the assets in Thailand and made a nice pot of money but now I will be looking to include the assets of her own and possible future assets as part of the divorce. This is a sign that she knows she has lost in Thailand.

The moral of this is don't be too greedy; tell your lawyer the truth and don't look a gift horse in the mouth. I believe that my wife lied to her lawyer both in Thailand and the UK. That has resulted in a lot of money being wasted and time.

I give the history of how we got to where we are and also go through what has happened in the UK and Thailand concerning the divorce; threats; false allegations; false claims and lies by my Thai wife and her family.

This book shows how greedy the Thai people can be and what lengths they are prepared to go for money.

There are 2 people I admire the most in History. It might explain my character is in some way. The 2 people are David Lloyd George and Wyatt Earp. David Lloyd George was the last Liberal party Prime Minister in the UK. I like him because he was from a poor background and was very left-wing and tried to help people - as Chancellor he introduced pensions in the UK. Wyatt Earp - he of the famous gunfight - was a very interesting character who was very tough but was intelligent and was clearly not prepared to run away from a fight.

The main characters in this farce. It is truly a farce as there are nonsensical and outrageous claims by people; manipulation; sexism; homophobic hate; and intelligent people thinking with their dicks rather than their brains. They are:

Myself – I will talk about myself later

My wife Somphorn (or Nicky or Nikki) Vale (or Tharaso)

John Hatfield – my wife's employer at one time who loves women from South East Asia and likes to be abused by them.

My wife's daughters – Ploy Laowanit and Lek. Both prepared to make false sexual allegations as they are Thai and that is what they do.

Pete Griffiths – a small-time crook in his youth who then changed his name to escape his criminal past. Of course, he didn't tell his employers about his criminal past when it came to vetting for jobs. He was found out once when the leisure centre he was working for was broken in to. He is a man who

likes to be the centre of attention and likes to control others –
that is why he doesn't like me and decided to lie.

The minor players - Mitesh Varsani (Mac) (the man who
hates gays and is definitely homophobic). My wife thought
that he would threaten and intimidate me. She forgot my
background as a child. As a child I lived on a tough local
government housing estate and was having a fight either at
school or out of school every week. A man like Mr. Varsani
would intimidate – I don't think so. He is a typical bully –
attacks in a crowd but then runs away when he is on his own.
He was a male escort as a teenager and he hates all older men
who he thinks are faggots. Yes, he still uses language like that
even though he is in his 30s p- I thought language like that
died out in the 1980s. As a child of the 60s and 70s I heard
language like that all the time in the school playground.

John Hatfield (the clown). This a man who loves South East
Asian women. He is well known for trying to have sex with
his Thai female employees at the Thai massage shop he owns

in Ruislip, West London (Sansara Massage Limited). As he is very weak the women get their revenge by borrowing money from him and then do a runner. He is too weak to take action to get the money back. My wife had a low opinion of him and sent me texts saying he was crying because the married business partner was not interested in him. That is probably the reason she has shares in both his companies. In some way he exploits the women who work for him as he pays them on a commission basis and does not comply with Employment Law in the UK.

Minor part - Ampol Tharaso (child rapist). A man who raped a girl of 8 in Thailand and yet my wife defends him while at the same time encouraging people to call me a faggot and a Jimmy Saville.

You always need a clown - did not Shakespeare always have a comedy character. Mitesh Varsani is the clown who makes some many moral somersaults that you wonder if he has any grip on reality. But definitely a damaged person.

My wife's (Somphorn Vale; Somphorn Tharaso; Nicky Vale; Nikki Vale) background was a poor one and a hard life in Thailand. She comes from a small town in Thailand near Chiang Mai. Chiang Mai is in the north of Thailand and so is cooler but is less developed than the capital city Bangkok. She was abused by her brother and did not see much of him as he was sent to the Temple to study to be a monk - which he failed at. He returned home and then raped an 8 year old girl and was sent to prison. I find this ironic that Mr. Varsani and Mr. Griffiths call me a pervert and a Jimmy Saville yet I have never been involved in anything criminal in my life and they know that my wife's brother has been involved in the rape of a child but refuse to condemn him. Interesting set of morals!

So we have the main characters; the stage is set; the players know their lines but the one important thing missing is the dress rehearsal along with some players not really knowing the plot of the play.

Chapter 2 : the courtship - the background to it all

I bet no foreigner has ever stood up in court in Thailand and refused to pay bail. I not only did it once but three times. I had packed my bag ready to go to prison in Chiang Mai in Thailand. The court was amazed and I was amazed and I was not amazed that no one believed me that I would volunteer to go to prison in Thailand. My own lawyer did not believe me before the court hearing nor did my translator. The lawyer asked me if I knew that I would go to Thai prison and he mentioned the name of a prison which, of course, meant nothing to me. I assume that it was a bad prison and that you didn't want to go there. I think he assumed that no foreigner would want to go to prison in Thailand.

The court was totally silent as the other lawyers in court and the judges could not believe it. Thai court is different from the UK. There are usually 2 or 3 judges and they are hearing different cases at the same time. The lawyers involved in the other cases are also in court. Everyone could not believe it.

Another lawyer said to my lawyer - I feel sorry for you your client has no money; my lawyer replied that I did have money. Outside the court, after the judge had let me go after asking me to promise to return in front of a picture of the King - which I did. I did not actually return to court – I returned to Thailand with no problems even though I had not complied with the bail conditions. I even obtained a visa!

I am now a legend in the court in Chiang Mai. A friend said to me that I was probably the only foreigner to ever stand up in court in Thailand and refuse to pay bail and not go to prison. There might be a course at legal school in Thailand about me.

Remember the prisons in Thailand have a terrible reputation. There are no beds and the prisoners are basically just locked in without any comforts such as a bed or a proper cup of tea or toilet paper or a bed or hot water or a proper western toilet – I think you get the picture. The worst thing for me would be no western toilet. I have been coming to South East

Asia for the past 15 years and I have still not worked out how to use a hole in the floor!. I can't work out the geometry or the physics of it. What do you do with your trousers; how do you sit without sitting; how do you get up? All the questions – I think if I had to use a South East Asian toilet all the time I would need some helpers.

In Thai prison that might not be a problem finding helpers. My wife once told me that if I ever went to prison that a ladyboy would be happy to look after me in prison. That to me sounds OK. If she is going to wash my clothes and look after me than I have no problem. Let's be honest a lot of ladyboys in Thailand look more beautiful and sexy than women. I have no problem with what people enjoy when it comes to sex. If people wanted to be naked all the time I have no problem with that. I don't understand why a lot of people want to proscribe what people can do and can't do in sex.

I had made the decision the night before as I had decided that I could use the money in prison to pay someone to sort out my problems with my wife and her family as they were trying to get me in prison. It also would be good for me as I would lose weight. Also living in squalor and dirt for a limited time doesn't concern me as I know it is only for a limited time. It would also mean that I lose weight! I would have gone through with it. I had emailed everyone – my wife; her Thai lawyer; my girlfriend and my Thai lawyer. I don't think anyone believed me. It might sound flippant but I had seriously thought about it. I had seen all the documentaries on TV and the Internet about Thai prisons. The maximum I could get in prison was 2 years but I was more likely to be deported and then I could come back to Thailand by paying a bribe to an immigration officer through an agent.

A note about Thailand. Thailand has immigration rules but you can circumvent those rules by talking to an agent and paying 100's of £s to an agent who then sorts out your immigration problem. The problem is so endemic that the British Embassy in Thailand is well known for being an easy touch for obtaining a visa to the UK by paying money to an agent. The agents guarantee a UK visa. It is well known that they can obtain a visa to the UK. In my experience that is a correct view. I paid an agent for my wife's daughter to get a visa to the UK and there was no problem. When I tried without an agent it was refused for the other daughter. Other people have had exactly the same experience with the British Embassy.

My wife has lied everything in Thailand in an attempt to get the assets in Thailand. She has come in a mob of 8 people to break into my home; she has tried to ruin my reputation by lying about me; she has told people to sort me out if I go to my home in Thailand; she has harassed my tenants in Thailand by sending them letters telling them to leave; she has sent people to talk to my tenants; she has stolen money from me; she has sold a house and a car I paid for in Thailand (don't worry the value of them will be recovered); she has sent family members who are local police officers to threaten me; she has sent police officers to look for me at my house in Thailand and more. She has also rewarded an Indian man from the UK who has been sending me messages for the past 2 years calling me a faggot and a pervert. (More about Mr. Varsani later). She has persuaded people to perjure themselves in sworn statements to the UK court.

I now have 3 arrest warrants in Thailand. I know this as 2 lawyers have told me this. These have been in place since the end of 2018. It is now at least a year later and I have been to Thailand on at least 3 visits since then. People were very concerned that I would get arrested so I did not go on a planned trip to Thailand in December 2018. Since the issue of the arrest warrants I have even spent an hour with immigration at the main Bangkok airport and no one has arrested me. I have been to Thailand a number of times and nothing has happened. Why haven't I been arrested; why when I go through immigration on entering Thailand do I not get arrested and why can I go to police stations and not be arrested. My theory is that the court in Chiang Mai has become fed up with the silly claims and lies of my wife and her family. The court realised that my wife is financing all the claims by her family against me and making silly claims. My wife and her family have upset the court as they don't turn up for claims or mediation. They also realise that I have been perfectly reasonable in my attitude towards the divorce and that I was very supportive of my wife's family. This is in contrast to the father of my wife's daughters who has provided no financial support; no home and no emotional support for his own daughters.

I am sure that some people would find this pressure intolerable. Not me – I enjoy the game. Everyone says to me that I am always cheerful. The main reason for this is that I find people funny and I find situations like this funny. A comedian once said that he only joked about the things that were important. I thrive on pressure. I always had a problem at the office if there was a long deadline for work to be done – I always left it until the last moment to do it. Without this sort of thing going on I might be bored. People who worked with me in the Metropolitan Police could see that in me. When something happens my 1st reaction is usually to say – Interesting. I hate people who panic. You are not dead so why are you panicking and you won't die from what is happening. I think that annoys people because they expect a particular reaction and they don't get it. I do find it difficult to empathise with people but I pretend to do so. I find it helps in social interaction and makes people think that I am nice. In reality I can't get upset about people's problems – I just pretend.

Women, I am in a relationship with, always comment that they never see me cry. It is strange. I am of a certain age that men were not encouraged to cry. I also come from the working class and men were taught not to cry. If you cried you were a cry baby or a sissy. Perhaps because I have been with women who are younger than me – my present girlfriend is 14 years younger than me. I am lucky – I will never deny that. From my background to what I can do now and what I have done means that I have had a good life even though I had such a bad start in life. As Jim Kirk states in Star Trek V that he would not want to change his life as it makes him who he is now. I agree with that. I am happy with me; I am happy with the life I have and I am happy with what I have done in my life.

My 1st wife said about me that I was the only person she knew that would be happy on a deserted island on my own. I think that is true.

I don't believe in ghosts; I don't believe in an afterlife; I don't believe in a God and I don't believe that there is a guardian angel. The one thing I do believe is that your date of death is pre-determined based on my experiences. I know that that is totally illogical but it means that I am prepared to take more risks in my life. There have been many times where car drivers in London have tried to kill me – at least once a year.

I have also had a couple of accidents over the years so I always take the view that whatever I do it will make no difference. If I go fast or slow on my motorbike it will make no difference as my death is predetermined. I think as a biker (motorbikes no bicycles) that we are all of the same view in some way or another.

How have I kept my sanity? Because of my background that has made me tough. I always take the view if 3 people attack me - then one of them is going down! I know how to be very violent but because of my background, I can be like that if I choose. That is another reason that I can look at things dispassionately, weigh up the consequences and then decide to take action that might result in some discomfort like Thai prison. Most Western people will pay thousands of £s to stay out off Thai prison but I decided after looking at what I could do in prison to take that option.

I like to do the unexpected - not to fall in with people's views about the best way forward. I will try to evaluate; look at the risks; the costs and then make my decision. Yes obviously that can sometimes be a bad decision but at least it is through my own actions and decisions not someone else's. Perhaps that is why I love motorbikes.

I have discovered that a lot of women love bikers. Why is that? After all most bikers are not modern men - they don't moisturise; they are not interested in women's problems and the nearest they come to emotional problems is when the girlfriend or wife is giving them grief. I think what attracts some women is that bikers are a relic from the past - the women like the shallow men whose main interest is motorbikes. The men are not complicated; they don't need validation; the men have high self-esteem; the men do not question their own existence; do not worry about women's things. Above all I think women love the hint of danger and risk and the possible menace lurking under every biker. It reminds women of the old knights and pirates. Only a theory but how many times do you see an old balding biker with a gorgeous woman riding bitch!?

You know I have had no problem finding pretty and sexy women. I am not handsome; I don't go to the gym every week; I don't eat salad (a lot) and I am not interested in the mechanics of your period! In fact, I think there should be a warning for men or a man filter when certain adverts for female products come on TV - I have no interest and will gain nothing from the information about your period as I don't have daughters and the information will not be useful in my own life - please talk to your female friends about that sort of thing. All the women that I have been with insist on telling me everything about their periods – why in heaven tell me and show me your period? Leave me alone.

So why have I never been on my own from the age of 18 - it can only be the motorbike! It is not money as I come from a poor background; it can't be my caring sharing attitude; it could be my big dick (women always complain that it is too big!) I just think that it is average. (Again I don't care if they are lying) and it can't be my knowledge of female problems! I come back to being a biker.

I have also decided that when this is over - the divorce is finalised then I will use all my financial muscle in Thailand to discredit the people involved - this book is part of that.

I also have another theory that there are a significant number of women in the world that do not want a man that is interested in being touchy-feely or crying all the time or knowing about moisturiser! Thankfully women also don't seem to make decisions about having sex with men based on looks. A lot of men would never have sex!. I have come to the conclusion that there is someone out there for everyone. I watch people a lot when I am out at a coffee shop or travelling or shopping. I am always amazed that there are beautiful women with very ugly men. I say thank you to women that being handsome is not the only criterion as I might have still been a virgin at 57!

I have a very good relationship with the court in Thailand. When I refused for the 3rd time to pay bail (without any consequence) I was asked by the court to go down to the holding area for prisoners - I was the only one there. The admin clerk was very apologetic and asked if I minded as it was expected while the judge signed the order to let me go. I have turned up for every mediation set up by the court and been very reasonable the whole time while my wife and her family have made the court very upset - including the admin staff. The main reason that the admin staff are upset is that they set up a Skype connection for my wife to attend mediation in the Thai court and at the last moment she changed her mind. Her daughter was told by the judge that she had to attend mediation and did not turn up - the judge was very pissed off.

I receive a warm welcome every time I go to court in Chiang Mai in Thailand. I don't think there are many foreigners who receive the same welcome as I do in a Thai court. What has helped is that the staff and judges have taken the view that I am a nice person. I supported very generously my wife and her family while the father (the 1st husband) has never provided any support whatsoever over 14 years and has children in another relationship who he does support. I have also been quiet and respectful towards the court. You need a lot of patience when you are in court in Thailand.

It is important to be patient; respectful and quiet in court in Thailand. Courts in the UK can be very noisy and confrontational. The courts in Thailand are the total opposite. My tip if you are in court in Thailand is this - it might seem slow and you might think that you are not getting your point across don't worry you will gain a lot of kudos for your quiet; respectful and patient demeanour. Don't forget to wear a good suit - they value that.

Why was I prepared to go to prison in Thailand particularly Bangkok? I had done some research. I had discovered that I might not be sent to prison but just deported. If that happened

I could pay an agent to get me a visa anyway to go back to Thailand.

Yes, you can do that. Even if you have been deported you can get a visa to return to Thailand. I was talking to my translator who also did visas. She told me the story of the man from Germany who was deported than he paid the immigration official to return to Thailand. The immigration official he paid to get the return visa was the same immigration official who deported him! Can you imagine that happening in the UK? I like Thailand! I understand it! I can work with that type of system!

I also discovered that the maximum prison term I would get was 2 years which meant that I would save money as I would not be paying rent or anything outside prison. I also realised that I could get out of prison by paying the bail money at any time. Also, I realised that the judges were reluctant to send people to prison because of the cost to the system. Finally, I could use my time in prison to recruit people to sort out my problems with my wife and her family. Therefore I calculated that it was unlikely I would go to prison but if I did then I could use the time to sort out problems and save money. The added bonus is I could make some useful friends in prison with the money that I have and I would lose weight. This would help my blood pressure as I have to take a tablet every day for it.

It is interesting that the court and the police in Thailand treated me fairly. This is in stark contrast to the police in the UK who have refused to take any action even though I had a non-molestation court order in place in the UK. The reason for the order was that my wife had informed people (one person in particular) that I was bisexual and this had caused him to send me many messages and to threaten me many times. It took many phone calls from my lawyer in the UK for the Met Police to take action after I was threatened by a friend of my wife in the street in London. There seemed to be a prejudice against a bisexual man from the police. I even showed them the messages and there was a metaphorical shrug of the shoulders from the police officer at Acton police station in London. The messages by any stretch of the imagination were hate mail but because I was a bisexual man they probably took the view that I deserved it. If I had been a crying woman I wonder what their reaction would have been with regard to the messages and threats?!

I was open about this to my wife; her family; her lawyer and the court in Thailand that I was going to spend the money to sort out my problems with my wife and her family. An ally of my wife said to me that he had been told that I had begged and cried to not go to prison. Anyone who knows me knows that would never happen. I mentioned this to a friend that this had been claimed and she laughed. She said the very same thing - that the people saying this clearly didn't know me. Particularly as I had been very clear that I was prepared to go to prison and not pay bail. I do not beg and would never beg.

Most people looking at me would see me as a typical tourist to Thailand. Old, balding and fat! I can live with that as most of the time I don't really care what people say about me. A manager in the Met Police once said to me that I was no fun as it was impossible to insult me and I replied - you can't insult me as I don't value your opinion! I don't value many people's opinion. I will seek people's opinion but I will then evaluate it by looking on the Internet or talking to other people. I would prefer that it was my mistake that results in my downfall rather than someone else's mistake or lack of knowledge. I find the intelligence of most people in the UK pretty low. Most British people whinge and moan but do nothing. They won't go on strike; they won't speak up and they won't use any intelligence to evaluate anything. I am glad I no longer live in the UK. Particularly after Brexit (it is still going on as I write this).

I would describe myself as a Gorilla. You know some people play that game of what animal would you be. I am similar to a gorilla but with brains. I can wait and can use language to get what I want. I can also be bloody difficult. I always try to do my research about a problem or the rules etc. A typical example of this is a delayed flight I had from London to Hong Kong and then I was going to have a 13 hour wait at Hong Kong airport for the flight to Xiamen (near Taiwan).

The flight was delayed when I was sitting in the boarding lounge. I don't mind that these things happen and anyway being British I am used to queuing. You queue everywhere in the UK. You queue at the doctors; in shops; at airports; at train stations; at work - customer service in the UK is a joke. The reason that it is a joke is that the British don't complain or when they do they just accept whatever the company tells them. So I suffer with the legacy of that as companies in the UK put up barriers to getting customer service as they know most British people just give up or accept what they are told.

Eventually, we are informed by Cathay Pacific that the flight has been cancelled. It only took them 2 hours to decide that.

They then had us collect our luggage and then put is in a queue to wait for news. After an hour they eventually decide to issue food vouchers as required under EU law. I timed how long it took to issue 1 voucher - it took nearly 5 minutes. At that rate it would have taken 1,500 minutes to issue food vouchers over 24 hours. Of course, being in the UK no one complains apart from me. I point out the amount of time it will take and I am told that is the process - after 45 minutes they give up on that idea. They then tell us a coach has been arranged to take us to Heathrow from Gatwick Airport, For those who don't know the airports then I will let you know that Gatwick is one side of London and Heathrow is the other. So we start meandering around Gatwick looking for a coach. In the meantime, I receive a text stating that I am booked on a flight from Heathrow in 90 minutes time. Not going to happen from Gatwick as we need to go on the notorious M25. I phoned Cathay Pacific Customer Service and was told "Oh don't worry you'll get there in plenty of time from Gatwick" Yeah right!

We find the coach and pile on. We have an hour now to get to Heathrow and for me to check in on the new flight. We get to Heathrow (after my new flight has left) and then placed in another long queue to rebook flights. Me being me goes to the front and in a very loud voice says to people "You do know that you are entitled under EU law to a leaflet explaining your rights; 600 Euros compensation and it is up to you what happens next!". Surprisingly a manager comes running out and says - "Ooh I heard you ask for a manager!" (No I didn't). He takes me to one side as says what would you like to happen? So I did not queue and I got a nice hotel for the night. This was not the end.

I am on the flight next morning to Hong Kong and I am 2 hours from Hong Kong and a female steward drops hot water on my lap! (Thank you God I thought - even though I am atheist). As I have said before accidents happen - it is important to me what happens next. If the organisation deals with the problem then no problem. However, as is usual when dealing with someone from the UK the organisation basically states that I can write to them and I will get a reply in about 28 days. So I have to sit in wet trousers at Hong Kong airport for 13 hours! Oh well, it gave me plenty of time to write my letter I suppose. Not going to happen.

I said to the flight manager that there were 2 ways the problem is dealt with - the hard way or the easy way. The hard way I arrive in Hong Kong and I go to the Hong Kong police and make a complaint of assault about the female steward or when I arrive at Kong the company sort out my flight. Guess which one they decided - yep they met me at Hong Kong airport and within 90 minutes I was on my new flight to Xiamen. Sorted because unlike the rest of my fellow citizens I show the organisation how bad it can be. This has been my attitude throughout my life - particularly when I was a Trade Union rep.

As I am impossible to intimidate it did not matter to me if I was dealing with a fellow accountant in the Met Police or the

Police Commissioner himself. I once argued with a Detective Inspector for 1 hour about the meaning of "must".

This came up as a result of a Gross Misconduct case where the staff member faced dismissal for getting a bit drunk on New Year's Eve and having an argument with the staff at a fast food takeaway. Yes, really gross misconduct! The case had been a joke from the beginning - she was suspended on full pay for at least 6 months; they sent 2 statements by her police officer manager one was signed the other wasn't; the manager had changed his recommendation after he had been talked to by Human Resources. They also then refused to allow me as the Trade Union rep to question the manager even though in the rules it stated that if a statement is used in a hearing then the person making the statement "must" be available for the hearing. The Detective Inspector stated (the Chair of the hearing) that I was not allowed to question the manager - so we argued for over an hour about the meaning of the word "must". I won the hearing in the end!

That is one example of how it is very difficult to intimidate me. I see my experiences bad or good as just another chapter of a book to learn from. I have been threatened physically and verbally and it does not matter to me. A red mist can descend if I let it.

That is one of the reasons I was able to understand my youngest son. He was born with dyspraxia and at some point a red mist would descend on him and no one else could control him. I understood where that red mist came from as I used to have it up until I was about 12 or 13 then I learned to control it. If I need to I can let that red mist descend and let it take over - when that happens it does not matter if you are bigger I am prepared to go all the way - there is no control; there are no limits and there is no regret. I control it and instead rely on words and rules and sarcasm to get what I want.

As I have got older I take more risks. When I was young I was afraid of most things. I think part of the reason for that is that I had to do everything myself. I had to sort out everything. I even at the age of 14 had to take my brother to Birmingham to the registry office for births deaths and marriages as my Dad had forgotten to add his middle name when he registered the birth. My fear of everything - heights; fairground rides; talking to people; asking for things; going to see people. I then started to change and decided I was being really stupid. After that I started to take more risks. I now take more risks than ever. I ride my motorbike at 120mph on the roads; I love roller coasters; I don't back down from confrontation (unless it gains me nothing). I am always analysing the risks and the gains that I can make. I always try to have a fallback plan.

However, looking back I did take risks. I would use construction sites as a playground in the evening when it was dark; I used to go off on my own on my bicycle without any money and cycle for hours all over the Midlands. I once had no brakes and there is a very steep hill in a place called

Stourport on Severn that ended with traffic lights at the bottom. I went all the way down it without any brakes and straight across the traffic lights. Fortunately, the lights were on green for me - Phew!

I used to go by motorbike every day to work - come rain; cold; sun or snow. Every year I could guarantee in London that someone would try to kill me. I only had 2 accidents in 25 years on a motorbike - and I have ridden motorbikes all over the world. The best accident, which was my fault, involved a new road laid where there were some loose stones on. I came too fast around the bend and slid. As I was sliding along the road still attached to the motorbike I was thinking how spectacular it looked and that I wished someone was filming as the sparks were flying from the exhaust as it dragged along the road. Another nearly accident involved a coach indicating right on the other side of the road suddenly decided to come across me. A woman on the side of the road who could see what was going to happen decided to scream.

As she did this I thought that is not much help! Fortunately, the coach driver saw me at the last moment and stopped and I was able to ride around the coach. No problem!

Getting back to my looks. I did not look like a gorilla when I met Nicky (her English name). When I met her I had a full head of hair and I also had a beard. I was thinner than I am now but all men when they reach 40 start to put on weight. I think this happens to every man – you put on weight; you lose hair and the hair in your nose and ears decides to grow very quickly each month! However, even though I am no beauty, I still have an order of importance that I tell all women I am in a relationship with. The four important things in order are:

1. My motorbike - the most important thing in my life. Your motorbike never lets you down! A motorbike never argues with you! And a motorbike always goes where you want to go! I have always loved motorbikes and have gone all over Western Europe

on my motorbike. I have also ridden around Uluru or Ayers Rock in Australia

2. My football club: I support Aston Villa and have supported them since the age of 9 - for nearly 50 years now. If you were to cut my bones you would find the club colours in the middle of my bones. I am claret and blue until I die. It is my local club as I am originally from Birmingham in the Midlands in the UK.

3. Tea: I can never go anywhere unless I have my English tea with me. Wherever I go in the world I take English tea with me (although it is from India, of course). I drink tea all day long. Thankfully when I worked for the Met Police it was free. I saved a fortune in not buying tea as I worked for them for 12 years.

4. Finally, any woman I am with. So if there was a fire in my home it is very clear what would be saved. It is important to get your priorities correct!.

I always say to people who know me that if I am in prison then they are to bring me the following:

1. Toilet paper - very important if you are English! Wherever you go in Asia there is never any toilet paper in the public toilets. Very annoying. In Thailand, they use a hose.

2. A mattress - this is to sleep on. I cannot sleep on the floor which some people still do in Asia. I am too old for the floor.

3. Tea - I need tea (see my comments earlier).

I always have this feeling or view that wherever I am I can arrange things to make my life more comfortable and easier. That I can bend the rules or change them for me. People always ask me how did you get that when it is supposedly not available. I feel that same if I were to go to prison in Thailand. I get on with people and can persuade them to do things or arrange things for me or get things for me. In China where I am now teaching, I manage to find bargains even though I can't speak Chinese.

I have an IQ of 144 to 146. I never know this until I was about 45. There were clues there. I took tests and would finish them before everyone else and score the highest mark - these are pseudo IQ tests. An agency once said to me after such a test that I had finished it more quickly than anyone else and scored the highest mark. In the end I took a couple of IQ tests and found out my score. I was a bit surprised and not surprised. Particularly after the other tests.

The reason that I can get other things people can't get in organisations is that I am good at understanding systems. As soon as I started my career as an accountant I discovered that I had a skill to quickly understand systems and to see their weaknesses. That is the reason I specialised in the setting up; review and improvement of company systems.

I also have been able to see the weaknesses in Government systems and use them to my advantage. One example of this is that under the Labour Government a system of giving money to families was introduced but it was based on your estimated income. If you earned above a certain level of income then you would lose these tax credits. The weakness was that you estimated your income for the next tax year but I soon realised that the Government did not check if the estimate was correct against your actual income. At that time I and my 1st wife were earning £200,000 per year between us but I would estimate my wife's earnings as about £20,000 for the following year. She was self-employed so income is not guaranteed but it was pretty well guaranteed. The reason that it was 90% guaranteed is because my wife was a School Inspector and that service had been privatised and subcontracted. Income was pretty well guaranteed as schools have to be inspected and there weren't enough Inspectors.

It is the same in any organisation that if you are clever enough you can use the rules to your advantage and see where the holes are in the system. I believe that as I have money I will be able to make life more comfortable for myself and also sort out the problems with my wife and her family. It is well known that the vast majority if not 100% of prisoners come from a poor background in Thailand. Offering money in prison to sort out problems outside prison will get you lots of offers of help. I said this in court and in meetings with judges at the court and no one told me that I couldn't say that. It was as if they understood the reason for doing this and approved of my views about my wife and her family.

My wife is very attractive. All men love her. I have seen it and I know. Someone once said to me do you know that your wife is flirting with men at a party we were at. In my view there are 2 outcomes: she comes home with me or she doesn't.

If she doesn't then she never comes home! It is over. I have a strong personality and a strong sense of self-worth. I always say that if you don't love yourself how can you love anyone else. I think that is very true.

My wife as I have said is very attractive and uses that to get what she wants. I think unfortunately for her it didn't really work with me. When she started to tell stories about me and make claims about me all the men went all misty-eyed and there protective instincts came out. My wife's skill at manipulating men had been honed when she was working as a prostitute. She makes a man think that she likes them and that she would do anything for them. I never fell for that but hey the sex was great. If your wife is giving you blow jobs and anal sex you are not too bothered - particularly when she is good at both. The 3somes were the best with my wife - I understand this is unusual for a Thai wife. My future wife would always ask if I wanted a 3some when I arrived at the brothel she was working at. My wife even arranged 2 massage girls at a local brothel to give me a soapy massage and then told the reception to arrange a taxi for me to get home when I had finished. My Thai wife also helped me pick out the girls.

Chapter 3 Some thoughts

Why did I decide to write this book? There are a number of reasons. I want to praise the legal system in Thailand. Surprising isn't it? Yet the Thai legal system has been more sensible; has actually evaluated evidence; has tried to mediate a solution and has upheld contractual rights.

It is always claimed that the Thai legal system is corrupt but I have not found that and I have been impressed by it. It has actually performed better than the UK system. I will come back to that later. I have found the Thai police to be helpful and only outside Bangkok have I found them to be corrupt. Outside Bangkok police officers seem to be from local families and so have loyalty to their community when it comes to outsiders and therefore will use their position in a corrupt manner. Only police in Chaing Mai stop me and ask for money while in Bangkok I have never been stopped under the same circumstances. I think that the police service in Thailand needs to move their police officers around or pay them more so that, in the provinces, they will not be too rooted in the local community such that they will ignore the law to help local people against outsiders. It is also easy to bribe local police officers. I will come back to that later.

I am also writing this book about my experience as I think it will help to redress the numerous videos on Youtube and books giving a gloomy and despairing view about divorce in Thailand. I have seen so many videos of men from the UK returning to the UK without any money as they have left their Thai wives. I think they gave up before they even started - they assumed that they had no rights in Thailand to assets. But this is a wrong view. If you have the paperwork - bank statements; bank transfers; emails etc you can keep the assets you have paid for in Thailand. Don't listen to all the other foreigners who state that you have no rights - this is not correct. You can keep all the assets you paid for. Thai divorce law is different to UK divorce as assets are dealt with in the following way:

1. If you brought assets into the marriage - you keep those assets

2. If you pay for assets during the marriage you keep the assets if the money came from your personal funds such as selling your property in the UK)

3. The rest of the assets are divided 50/50

So if you are a foreigner in Thailand married to a Thai person then you should get 50% of the assets if not 100% as you can get financial records from banks etc to show you paid for those assets. That is what I want foreigners to understand - don't believe the stories.

If you are very organised and had a lease contract put in place or kept the original records then you can claim the assets in the marriage. Most foreign people forget that they have a claim against assets held by the Thai person as they are probably poor so you paid for them anyway and if they were bought during marriage then you can make a claim.

A lease contract is a way in South East Asia of recognising a foreigner's rights to their investment in land. Foreigners in South East Asia cannot own land so a way around this is to set up a lease contract for a maximum of 30 years with a promise in it to grant another 30 years. You can own a flat or apartment outright as there is no land. You can also set up a company to own the land but you need a Thai as a majority shareholder. At the time I bought the house in Thailand I set up a lease contract and a loan contract. The loan contract stated that I had lent the money to my wife to buy the house and that this would be repayable. At the time of setting up the loan contract, there were no restrictions on the length of a loan but the Supreme Court in Thailand put a maximum period of 10 years on a loan so I can't enforce that part now as it is more than 10 years.

Foreign people are also concerned about being killed as this has happened in Thailand to foreigners. There are many examples of Thai women cutting the cock off husbands who have an affair. This is done while the husband is asleep. Can you imagine it? Also, the women have been known to get their family to attack the foreign husband. That is a risk anywhere but I will admit that there is a higher risk in Thailand. It depends on you with regard to that. I come from a tough background so my view is that you want to attack me physically then I will hurt you badly. I think that this comes from my background and I am also a biker (motorbikes not bicycles!). My wife learned this - read about it later!

As I said I am old, fat and balding - shouldn't I be scared of going to prison in Thailand and do anything to avoid it? I read in the UK that a young English person paid £20,000 to avoid prison in Thailand. I am also 57. Not young but with a stubborn streak. I tend to evaluate the risks and the probability of the bad side happening. I came to the conclusion that it was worth the risk and send a message to my wife; her family and the courts. It worked! My lawyer was astounded.

My plan was and is the following if I ended up in prison in Thailand. The first day I would make sure I knew where everything was and the routine - when food; when showers and so on. The second day I would find a Thai person in prison who could speak English. The great thing about the English language because of the dominance of the USA economy and the British colonial era is that you can find someone who speaks English anywhere in the world. I always tell my students when I am teaching them English. The English language is very useful because you can find someone, anywhere who can speak English. I have been all over the world and this has always been true. I have been all over Europe; China; Vietnam; Cambodia; Laos; Thailand; South America; the Arctic Circle; Africa and always found someone who speaks English. It makes the English very bad at speaking other languages. I can, however, speak Thai as well.

Someone said to me that I was the only person they knew that could look upon a time in a Thai prison as a positive thing. People often ask me why I am always cheerful. There are a number of reasons - one is my background, if you come from where I come from then you would be cheerful about your present life and I always have a plan. I can never take much in life seriously. Some would argue that I have never had bad things happen to me - but they have. I have been fired 3 times; I have been homeless with my family and I have been penniless but throughout it all, I remain cheerful. I take the view that I am still alive which is a bonus.

I have always said that I want to live to be the oldest British man. The main reasons for this are that I want to get my money's worth from UK pension after the crash of 2008 the British Government increased the age I retire; made the pension more expensive to contribute and reduced the pension to give to the Bankers in the UK. The other reason is I want to say to the British people when they come to interview me - they always do if you are the oldest British man or woman still alive - that the reason I have lived so long is because I fucking left the UK when I was 50; I love sex and I love meat. I have always wondered if they will continue to play Vera Lynn music from the 2nd World War to my generation in care homes in the UK or play Glam rock and Rolling Stones. I read that a man in a care home in America was kicked out as they found him in bed with 2 prostitutes one morning. I don't get that but then that is America. The land of the stupid; racist and creationist idiots, Did you know that in surveys they find that at least 45% of people in America believe in creationism! Crazy but true.

If you are not British or not lived in the UK you cannot underestimate the fascination of the British with the 2nd World War. It is as though time stood still in 1945. Politicians still mention the war; newspapers keep mentioning the war and British people still talk about the Germans wanting to take over Europe. I was not born during the war; even my parents were only 10 when it finished. Can someone tell the British the war ended in 1945 can we move on in 2019! I am fed up with it.

My brother is not a half-full kind of guy. People always ask me if we come from the same family. He has not optimism; no drive; no curiosity. It is as though all the life has been taken from him. He is a person waiting for something to happen while I want to make it happen. If I see a hill I want to know what is on the other side. My brother would worry that you could get killed climbing the hill or that you will ultimately be disappointed when you reach the top of the hill. His ultimate insult for me is that I am an adrenaline junkie. I will take that as I don't see that as an insult.

I always find it amazing that people don't think like me. The possibility of going to prison in Thailand did not make me prepared to do anything to NOT go but I looked at the problem in a logical way – looked at the potential downside and the possible upside. I think this comes from my half-full glass mentality. It enables me to look at the problem rather than overreact to the potential risk only. Like going to the Bangkok Hilton as prison in Bangkok is known as. I have no idea who started that joke about prison in Thailand but prison in Thailand is nothing like the Hilton!

Yes, I have a Thai wife and a Thai girlfriend. Both very pretty. How do I do it? I have never worked it out. I was terrible with women when I was young and I don't consider myself that attractive. Someone asked me if I had a giant cock. I don't think so but all the women I have had sex with have never said – well size doesn't matter – all of them have said that I have been too big. I think I am just average – thank God women are no good at estimating the size of things. Also, I am very happy that women are not like men – just interested in beauty. If they were, most men would not have a girlfriend or a wife.

The only success I had with women was at teacher training college. I went in 1980 and the college had only just become co-Ed. This meant that the ratio of women to men was 8:1 – what a place. Even I scored and never stayed in my own room the whole year. I left after a year as I did not see myself teaching the history of the cold war since 1945 to the bottom set of History for the rest of my life. Mind you I did meet my 1st wife there.

I stayed with my 1st wife for 23 years and I have been with the Thai wife for 12 years – so I have been married for a total of 35 years. I don't think that is a bad record. I was still with my 1st wife when I met the Thai woman.

Getting back to my moment in the Thai court. You have to remember that court cases are not held one at a time but you have 3 or 4 going on at the same time with 2 or 3 judges presiding.

When my translator announced that I refused to pay bail the whole court stopped. The judge asked for my lawyer to explain but he couldn't so the judge asked me through my translator. I stated that I could afford the bail (which I could) but I felt that the money would be better used if I was to pay prisoners to sort out my problems. The judge thought for a moment and decided to ask me if I would swear in front of the King's portrait to return – to which I agreed. There were no other restrictions placed on me and I kept my passport. Then I was free to go. I am now a legend in the Thai courts in Chiang Mai. I have done it 3 times and never had any problems leaving the Thai court. Did not pay any bail money; did not surrender my UK passport and did not have any restrictions placed on me.

So how did I manage in a criminal case against me in Thailand as a UK national manage to walk out refusing to pay bail and effectively stating that I was going to get prisoners to sort out problems with my Thai wife and her family. I even stated to judges in mediation with judges at the court that I was never going to pay a penny in fines or pay a penny in bail. Can you imagine if I stated that in a US court – I would go straight to prison. The reason that I was not sent to prison in Thailand is that the judges had worked out why my wife and her family were using the criminal courts to attack me.

To help in the understanding of the court system in Thailand I will explain a few things to help your understanding. The Thai legal system is different from the West in that lawyers can bring criminal complaints on behalf of their clients. This is clearly different from the West. Also, lawyers in Thailand can bring criminal complaints to put pressure on defendants to pay money as the reputation of the prisons are so bad in Thailand. Also, the Thai legal system loves mediation. I have attended so many meetings with the judge that I have lost count. Overall I have had a good experience with the Thai legal system – they have seen through the real agenda of my wife and her family and have refused to send me to prison even though I have refused to cooperate in open court.

It has been a different experience in the UK. The UK courts have bent over backwards to assist my wife in her claims. It has been to such an extent that I have not been allowed to challenge her sworn statements. There has been an attitude both from the UK police and the UK courts and I can only put it down to the fact that there it is based on gender and/or my sexuality.

I saw this attitude in the Metropolitan Police. I was an accountant and a trade union representative – I eventually ended up as President of the Union in the Metropolitan Police. I saw the attitude of some police officers towards gay men and it was appalling. One gay man was treated so appallingly by a Police Officer manager that when the Metropolitan Police eventually admitted that it had treated this man wrongly, he would at meetings crawl under the table and start to cry. The work that Sir Ian Blair had all gone after he left as a lot of experienced police officers still carried the prejudice of the 1950s. The changes that Sir Ian Blair disappeared overnight.

The reason they disappeared is that after Ian Blair was sacked or resigned then the next Commissioner (Bernard Hogan-Howe) brought a sigh of relief from Police Officers as he had been involved with the Met Police before. He was seen as a friend of Police Officer and would stop all this nonsense about equality; stopping racism; stopping misogynistic behaviour and stop the transfer of jobs from Police Officers to Police Staff.

There are some good Police Officer managers but they are few and far between in the Met Police. It would be very difficult for a Police Officer in the Met Police to be promoted as they would be considered to have the wrong attitude. I did meet some of them and it is a pity that the reforms introduced by Ian Blair and his predecessor were dropped very quickly after Hogan-Howe became Commissioner. A good example of this is that a policy was introduced to take disciplinary action against disabled staff which ultimately led to their dismissal on attendance grounds. The manager would always state that they knew that more absence would occur because of the disability of the staff member but the Commissioner Hogan-Howe had made the decision. I found that attitude disgusting on a number of fronts. The first was the abdication of responsibility by the manager - they were basically saying that they were only following orders (the Nuremberg defence) and secondly I found it disgusting that an organisation in a so-called civilised society is targeting disabled staff in such a way. But this summed up the Met Police - all staff Police Staff and Police Officers have been in the organisation too long and have lost all sense of morality because that behaviour was rewarded by the organisation with promotions and benefits.

Throughout my career I have never supported anything that was immoral such as that policy. I have spoken up even though it has not been popular and I have opposed any policy that was designed to discriminate and attack people in an organisation. Allied with my knowledge of the rules I was very effective as a Trade Union rep. I was known as the Bob Crow of the Met Police and I always felt that the only weapon left to the working class and employees is the strike weapon. This was proved by Bob Crow. Bob Crow was infamous in the UK as he was the leader of the Transport Union in London. He, with the help of his members, raised the pay of London Transport staff immensely so that drivers on the London Underground could earn £50,000 per year. Everyone hated him - the national newspapers and commuters in London.

It is interesting the difference between France and the UK. In France when the transport unions went on strike about the planned increase in the pension age to 60 and caused major problems for everyone in France particularly commuters in Paris the strike received support from the people of France. France 24 the English speaking French news channel undertook polls of people's support for the strike - there was overwhelming support for the strike. I always said to Union members in the Met Police if you want to get anything then you have to take it. Arthur Scargill, leader of the NUM (National Union of Coalminers) once said that an organisation will only give what the employees are prepared to take. The only way was to go on strike. Members in the Met Police would not go on strike which is the same for most people in the UK and that is why the UK has the worst pensions in Western Europe and starts to receive pensions at a later age than anyone else in Western Europe.

I am however more complex than that. I am right-wing on certain subjects and I am left-wing on others - which would be the same as most people. I would shoot the Royal Family in the UK if I could but at the same time I don't think it is incumbent for companies or individuals to pay more tax than the Government in a country has set. I find it quite ridiculous that people in the UK criticise the online traders for not paying enough tax even though they are paying the tax set by the British Government.

Prejudice and discrimination are rife in the Met Police and there is no impetus to deal with it.

I met this prejudice first hand when I tried to enforce the non-molestation order against my wife in the UK. At first, they could not find it then the police officer responsible denied he was responsible. The police actually lied to my lawyer – it was only after 3 weeks of constant phone calls by myself and my lawyer did they enforce the non-molestation order. The Metropolitan Police still an old fashioned view of harassment!

The courts in Thailand have seen through Mrs. Vale's game. They have seen so many Thai women try to claim that they have paid for everything – house; car; living expenses even though it is impossible for them to do so as they don't have the income or resources. The Thai women are spurred on by men from the UK who just give up. The men think that because they are from the west they have no rights in Thailand – however as I have discovered everyone has rights in any country that respects contract and property rights. The

Internet is full of horror stories of English men leaving Thailand with only a suitcase of clothes and no money while the Thai woman keeps all the assets – the money; the cat and the house.

The horror stories I have seen on the Internet of foreign men in Thailand losing everything when they are involved with Thai women inspired me to write this. Foreign men losing everything and being attacked. Houses being demolished and transported to another location.

It was fortunate that I had my wife sign a lease contract and had the original bank transfers to prove that I had paid the money for the house from personal money.

The divorce laws and the court system are different in Thailand. If you can prove that you brought assets into the marriage or purchased assets using personal money that those assets are yours on divorce and you do not have to give your wife a share of them. If you can't prove that or you bought assets together then if you can't agree then in divorce court they are divided 50/50.

This has caused a problem for my wife as I can prove the assets were bought using my personal money from assets I solely owned in the UK. If she wanted a share of then she needed to buy me out. This she did not want to do so she came up with the idea of calling me a paedophile and made the claims that I wanted to have sex with her daughter.

Regardless of the fact that I could claim all the assets in Thailand, I offered her 50% of the assets and the judges in Thailand backed me up.

Chapter 4 The real beginnings?

I do not know exactly when she decided to tell people these things about me but I do know that it was before August 2017 but I suspect it was in January 2017 that it started as she left for the UK in February 2017.

She told me that she was leaving as she was bored in China and she didn't like staying in China anymore. We were in China as I decided to leave the UK as I could not see any future working in the public sector. You have to remember that the Lib Dem/Conservative had introduced a pay freeze and increases in taxes and increases in the pension contribution to the Civil Service pension scheme while reducing the redundancy terms on offer as a result of the 2008 financial crash. Interestingly the bankers who caused the crash and reduced everyone's pension in the UK kept their bonuses and pensions. I engineered my redundancy from the Metropolitan Police as I could see that the pension would get worse and the redundancy terms would get worse.

As I was over 50 I could take a reduced pension. I left the Metropolitan Police just after I had been elected President of the Trade Union for Police Staff. I am sure I was the Police worst nightmare – but that is another story.

My wife did not at any point state that she did not want to go to China and seemed to agree with the plan to work for another 5 years and then retire as I would eventually have 3 pensions for the rest of my life. This would be more than enough to live in Thailand where I planned to retire.

I had financed the purchase of a house in Thailand out of my 1st divorce as I received £350,000 from that divorce. I had bought the house so the money was locked away and I would have my housing needs looked after when I retired and would have no costs such as rent or mortgage in retirement. It looked as though everything was set fair for the future. Perhaps that is the time that life hits you over the head to remind you that nothing is certain in life.

We met 13 years before. I was in the process of leaving my 1st wife and I met the new wife as she was working as a prostitute in London. Like many Thai women she had come to the UK as she needed money as she came from a poor family. She was very good at her work. Every time I came to see her she offered me a 3some with another girl. She also many other things as well. She worked all over London and was very popular.

I find it ironic that my wife is accusing me of all sorts of things when she was involved in some very strange sexual practices. She was involved in 3somes with other women; she e gave oral sex to men and women; she pissed on men;' she kicked men in the balls for 30 minutes to an hour (I can't imagine – the pain would be too great); she shit into a plastic bag so a customer could eat it; and so many more things. She was very popular and she told me that her record for sex was 10 men in one day!

Then she goes around telling people that I am a pervert!

She began to see me outside work and offered me sex at no charge. I started to see her at the various places she was working – I saw her at her place of work in Stratford, East London and Hanwell in West London. I then started to visit her at her home Wood Green in North London. She lived in a house with other Thai women who were involved in prostitution. It was an old house and I could see it was overcrowded and was clearly making the owner a fortune as they were mainly illegal Thai women with no status in the UK and the owner knew this.

You might ask why I started having unprotected sex with a prostitute. Firstly I have to say that I am a risk-taker and secondly she was very serious about her personal hygiene. She would never have unprotected sex with anyone else (I believed her); only Eastern European women at that time were offering bareback sex (or unprotected sex) and she had regular checkups. All the Thai women had regular checkups – at that time people were still dying from AIDS and the drugs available now weren't available then. She did have

standards – she would not have anal sex with someone whose

cock was too big (or a size she would not want to try). I don't

think there were too many men who came into that category.

However she would do any sex for money – she has had

3somes with me and another prostitute; she has pissed on

men; she has given oral sex; anal sex and pussy sex to lots of

men over a period of 2 years; she has kissed both men and

women; she would supply any type of sex and other women;

girls and boys for money. To my wife, at that moment, he did

not matter what you wanted – she would supply it, even

drugs.

I would talk with the women she lived with and I quickly

became an expert in the sexual services being offered in

London and the price of such services. Was I disgusted by it –

not at all, just curious. I met the women where she lived as I

would go and stay with her on a Wednesday night each week

as Thursday was her day off. I stayed at the house where she lived with other Thai woman and all of them had come on false passports and bought their visas from the British Embassy. They had all paid £26,000 (approx.) to an agent who then paid the British Embassy. The British Embassy was the easiest place to buy a visa. The £26,000 was a loan that they paid off when they came to the UK. What I never understood and never asked is why did they pay it off? You could just ignore it as you are in the UK. I think the reason they paid it off – and I know they did as I went to parties where Thai women were celebrating paying off the loan – was that the Thai community is very close and what you don't do in the UK has repercussions in Thailand. I would imagine that their families were threatened.

I never did ask her whether she did pay off the money before she was deported.

She would arrive between 6pm and 7pm from work. The basic charge for sex was £50 this gave you 30 minutes but most men only survived about 10 minutes. For 2 women you would pay £90 (a small discount). If you wanted the 2 women to have sex with each other then it would be £120. For other services such as anal sex or to see the girl swallow your cum then it was about £140. If you worked as an escort i.e. visiting the clients then you could charge more. The problem is that it was more dangerous.

Talking about dangerous. The reason that my wife's friend stopped working in the brothel business as a maid was because it was becoming more dangerous. There were men going to flat sin London late at night (near closing) and producing a gun or knife to steal the money. Women have died as a result of being shot in brothels during thefts.

The role of the maid was to be the manager of the brothel. A typical brothel was in a flat or a small house. The brothel would have 3 girls working there normally. The maid's role was to answer the phone, sell the girls' attributes; find out what the man wanted; give him the prices and give the address. When the client came to meet and greet them. The maid also looked after the money and made sure that everyone got their cut. The way the money was divided was in a particular way. Out of the £50 basic fee – the maid would receive £10 the house or flat owner would receive £20 and the girl would get the rest £20. So the girl would make £20 so was keen to upsell to other services – 2 girl or anal sex or swallow as they would keep more of the money per customer. Brothels then advertised in the local paper or in phone boxes in Central London. Of course, now it is on the internet. This has increased competition and I have heard that in some places you can get sex for £10 now.

It does not matter what people do – my view is that it is up to them. I am fed up in the UK with the need for people to judge and try to tell people what they should and shouldn't do when it comes to sex. I call it the Anglo-Saxon disease - this preoccupation with sex; drugs and roll. Throughout the history of the UK and the USA there has been a problem with the three main pleasures of life. So many laws have been passed to limit or ban all three. There has been a different story in Europe which started with Ancient Greece.

Chapter 5 : Who am I?

I am sure you are wondering. They say that I was born in a lucky generation – as I was born in 1962. I have to admit that what I received as a child and teenager was much more than today's generation. However, we did work hard and I have paid a lot of tax and helped to generate a lot of wealth for the UK so I have more than repaid the amount that was invested in me by the UK. I was also born at a lucky time as society was changing. Without those changes, I would not have had the opportunities I have had or the chance to be looking forward to a comfortable retirement. I have taken full advantage of the opportunities given to me. Mind you there was only one way as I couldn't really go any further down from my childhood.

I was born into a household and had parents who were typically working class. They came from a family that had always been working class and I am sure if you go back far enough you will see that my family would have been peasants. My very name suggests that.

I am from the Midlands in the UK – specifically Birmingham which is an industrial town. Surnames in the UK are usually based on a craft or job – so Fletcher was a maker of arrows and Thatcher made the thatched rooves in the UK. Vale is a generic which just means lives in a valley – so no skill or occupation: therefore a peasant. My parents were very typical 60's working-class – my father worked in the car industry on the production line and my mother stayed at home to look after the family. One good thing is that, as far as I know, my family has never died for their country. My family has managed either to ignore the call to save the UK or has been in a reserved occupation. I certainly know that one of my grandfathers was in a reserved occupation during the 2nd world war. I certainly take the same view that I will never get involved in any war for the British – I certainly support the view that patriotism is the last refuge of the scoundrel or the liar. This has certainly been true when it came to the Iraq war – weapons of mass destruction, really!

It amazes me that at that time, and still sometimes do today, working-class people had rituals about holidays and food. For instance, on each weekday I knew what I would have for dinner – if it was Thursday it would be fish fingers, Chips and Beans and my parents continue this to this day. It is so ingrained that my parents will have fish and chips on Saturday even if it is Xmas day. The working class also tended to go to the same place for holidays every year. My brother has continued this tradition – he goes to the same place for a holiday every year. This is Weymouth.

Weymouth is a small seaside resort on the South coast of England. I think it has pretensions of being an upper-class beach destination in the UK. It is quite small but pleasant – certainly better than Blackpool. Now Blackpool is the pits. I have been to both and I prefer Weymouth. My brother must like it as he has been going there for 20 years – camping as well. I don't camp anymore. I am of an age when I like my creature comforts. It also reminds me of when I was young – too many cold nights in a caravan with no heating. When I went to Weymouth with my brother I knew more about Weymouth than he did and he had been going there for 20 years!. I do my research even though it appears that I don't.

My brother has 2 daughters. I admit that I don't understand women and that I could be considered a Neanderthal by some women. However, they are slightly wrong about me. I am not interested in knowing about periods or female problems; I did not enjoy the birth of my children – I would have felt happier waiting in a waiting room like in the 1960s but instead, the midwife says to me "Mr. Vale you can see the head" "No thanks" "Oh yes really come and see" they had to drag me there to look at this bloody mess and the top of a head looking at me from the birth canal! Not pleasant. There should be a man filter on TV when certain products come on TV. As a man, there are certain things and information I have no use for as I will never use the information or know the products.

I was working with a woman when I first came to China to teach in 2016. She was in her 50s; had a chip on her shoulder about not having a degree; men and had a white guilt so she actively sought out Black men as she blamed white men for all her problems in life. As you can imagine she loved me! She was on her own at that point. On the 2nd night she got drunk and let slip that she had brought her favourite vibrator with her and had a special name for it. She arrived after we had been in China for a couple of weeks. Her name was Lynne Langdon.

Continuing the story of who I am. My family were very poor until we moved to a council house when I was 7. I thin that saved us from a life of homelessness. I remember having to move to my grandparents and living with them over Xmas one year – I can only imagine that we were there as we had nowhere else to live. We lived in a caravan for 2 or 3 years I think from the age of 5 to 7. It had no heating apart from a wood stove and had no bathroom. The shower block was a walk across an open field. My parents never understood how government systems worked and had no control over money. It was fortunate that we moved into a council house. People have said to me I should write the story of my life as I have lived enough for 2 lives – I have been a hacker; accountant; entrepreneur; trade union President and English teacher in China. I also have an IQ of over 140 but I only found that out when I was 40! I love to

My childhood was hard. I had no support from my parents and I don't remember being tucked up in bed or stories being read to me as a child. I never remember any cuddles. I do remember having a teddy bear but at the age of 5 or 6 it got burnt by my mother – I don't know whether that was deliberate or an accident. After that, I never wanted another teddy bear after that. I had no books as a child apart from comic books. I only started to read proper books after I went to school and started to buy books for myself or borrowed from the library. I have a love of reading which continues to today. I don't know where that came from as I never saw my parents read apart from daily newspapers and they were the more sensational lowest common denominator newspapers. They read papers like the Daily Mirror (and still do) and News of the World. There was no in-depth analysis of the issues of the day. Fortunately, at that time there were excellent documentary programs on TV. They covered in-depth subjects such as the Pol Pot in Cambodia; the Vietnam War; homelessness in the UK with "Cathy Come Home" and others.

It was a tough background which probably made me tough emotionally. I always had a curiosity about things. So, if as a family, we went anywhere new I would be the 1st to find out where everything was on the 1st day.

At the age of 5 to 7 I remember living in a caravan – Americans would call it a trailer park – it was not pleasant.

No heating and no bathroom. The TV worked on a car battery and used to run out of power at about 8pm. I remember the power cuts in the early 70s – it was a great excuse not to do your homework as you just said to your teacher that there was a power cut and they had no way of knowing where power cuts were. The power cuts were due to the strikes that were going on at the time against the proposed income policy of the Government. I Also remember a bread shortage – I queued with my father outside a store to pick up 2 loaves of bread each. At one point there was also a sugar shortage. Unthinkable nowadays – if people are without there mobile phone for a couple of hours it is purgatory for people now. I remember a time before mobile phones. There was no way you could contact someone if you were late or delayed. Most public phone boxes were vandalised; not working or you lost your money and it didn't connect.

I didn't realise we were poor as there was nothing to measure it against. We were not interested in the latest trainer and we only had limited glimpses of the world – there was no internet and there were only 3 channels available on the TV. Big events in most working-class families was getting the 1st colour TV set or staying in a hotel on holiday. I remember getting the 1st colour TV set in our house. I was not told the night before as the black and white TV set was moved out of the lounge. I had no idea what was happening. I only found out the next day when I cam home from school and the new colour TV set was there. It was amazing. I think I was 10 at the time so it would be 1972. The TV set was rented as most did then.

They were limited horizons and only the small things changed. I once saw Saturday Night Sunday Morning film and that was an excellent reflection of life. Being in the working class was harsh but at least life was improving for the working class as all political aims had the aims of building cheap homes and reducing poverty. The working class did benefit as there was free dental; free specs; and free access to University. I even received money for living from the Government. However, the world was changing so much that eventually it left the working class behind and ultimately they were ignored by the political parties.

My parents did not understand the changing world and still don't. My father still reads the same newspaper as he has always done – it amazes how long it takes him to read the paper – I can read it in about 15 minutes – it takes him the whole day. I quickly understood this new world and at times have done very well. Unlike other people who have escaped these conditions, I do not look down on those that were left behind nor do I despise them. I just think they have been abandoned with no alternatives being offered to replace the hard manual jobs that used to be done by the working class. They cannot learn how to become IT network support or sell mobile phones or do data entry. Without Government support and benign neglect on the part of the Government I would not have succeeded – I would have ended up working on the production line at British Leyland. This was the limit of my parents' ambitions as they did not realise that the world was changing and that you not only needed to look at today's horizon but all the future horizons.

This is my 2nd marriage which is different from my brother and my parents. My parents have been married for nearly 60 years. I have no idea if they love each other or that there was any passion about their marriage. They often say that children repeat the errors of their parents. I have tried to avoid that.

My brother and my parents are totally different from me. I am outgoing and ambitious and curious – they have none of that. My brother still lives in the same small town as when we 1st arrived when he was 5 years old. He has no ambition to see the rest of the world or to work in the nearest big city (Birmingham). He could certainly obtain more money but the problem is also that he has never improved his skills in IT. I have more skills and knowledge in IT than he does even though I have been an accountant most of my working life.

I think this background has made me more prepared to take risks and not to be too worried about money. I have ensured that I am secure for the rest of my life but I do not obsess about it. I look for solace in other things. I adhere to the view that even if everything is fucked I have still got my motorbike. My motorbike is my only love. I love women and ladyboys equally.

I forgot to mention that I am also bisexual - I love ladyboy cocks but I don't love men. I love women and ladyboys. I only started to love both from the age of about 40 and have loved them ever since. I have tried most things when it comes to sex and have no problem with people who like the more exotic side of sex. Most men would not say that they were bisexual even though they have sex with ladyboys in Thailand. I once watched a series of programs on British TV about British men who have long term relationships with women in Thailand. They state that they are not gay or bisexual but at some point there must be contact with the ladyboy cock and the ladyboy must cum. I think ladyboys make sex complicated because they look like an incredibly beautiful woman and they behave like women. Most have their cock still but have had breast enhancements and other improvements.

I heard a famous story in Thailand once. It might be an urban myth – who knows. The story is that a British man came to Bangkok and went out partying in Nana. Nana is the main area for picking up ladyboys in Bangkok. He went drinking and sometime during the evening made an arrangement with a bar girl to go back to his hotel room. The next morning he wakes up and realises that the bar girl was really a ladyboy (pre-op – still has everything a man has). I think most men would say to themselves this never happened and I will erase from my memory tape and never mention it again. This man wanted his money back and the ladyboy calls the police. When the police arrive she states that she is not giving the money because the British man enjoyed himself at least twice during the night. This got into the national newspaper in Thailand. Not a good move on the part of the British man.

I met my 1st wife when I was 18 when I went to teacher training college. She was 4 years older than me and if I had been more experienced would have not continued to go out with her. She was an only child and like a lot of only children she had never had to compete with a sibling; share or be independent. Also she had elderly parents as she had been born when they were in their 40s. She was also handicapped by her parents as they lived their lives through their child.

They reminded me of the book by George Orwell "Coming up for air". They were originally working class but had become lower middle class as the father worked in the civil service and the mother worked as a school secretary. They aspired to be upper middle class as their daughter had obtained a scholarship to an expensive private school in London. I think that this was the worse thing that ever happened to their daughter as she always had a chip on her shoulder as she always felt inferior to them and became obsessed with money.

The other thing that did not help was their obsession with food. Her parents had gone through the war and rationing and they had this fear or dread that they would run out of food. They had a store cupboard which was totally inadequate. If there had been a war then the food would have lasted at the most a week or 2 weeks. It was totally irrational. The parents of my 1st wife sent her for horse riding lessons (after all that is what the upper class in the UK love). They then sent her for ice skating lessons with a well known professional trainer. My wife also insisted we had a store cupboard – was a war imminent (I don't think so).

This all affected our relationship as a married couple as we were never left in peace. Every holiday we had to be with her parents – Xmas; New Year; Easter and summer holidays. I am not just talking about visiting but actually living with them or staying in the same room on holiday. It was ridiculous. I did put my foot down about going to Scarborough in the North of England every summer.

Scarborough used to be a popular holiday town about 100 years ago and then it was all downhill. It did not have much going for it and as far as I could see it had no redeeming features to it. It is also in the North of England in the county of North Yorkshire. They speak with a strange language and have some strange ideas. The reason we were in Scarborough is that my 1st wife and her parents went every year to visit her Aunt.

I could not stand it. We had to be in bed by 10pm and were not allowed a key. There was no heating allowed and we were not allowed to use the washing machine. My wife's aunt, we were staying with, even used next door's washing machine to wash – too stingy to buy her own machine. The thing was she was not poor as she was a retired teacher on a full pension in Scarborough – Scarborough must be one of the cheapest places to live in the UK. Mind you you couldn't pay me to live there! Scarborough is not warm in summer in one of the back streets of the city. I am not a snob. I like fish and chips; I like sitting on the beach in my socks and a knotted handkerchief on my head and I will even eat fish finger sandwiches with a lot of sand in them. I would not mind living on a council estate as that is where I am from. However I draw the line on being told that I can't do my washing as it would offend her Aunt who won't allow us to use her washing machine. There was no way that I was going back there for a miserable 2 weeks every year.

And it was miserable and usually rained as I went there for 3 years. Every day was the same. Get up and walk down to a beach hut facing the North Sea with the cold wind whistling from it as you sat huddled around the small stove trying to gather some warmth from its pitiable heat. All they wanted to do (including my wife) was to play cards and moan about socialists while they had they received free health care and pensions. Typical British people. Thank God I have left. Can you imagine how bad the UK is now for retired people – a lack of Government social support and listening to Vera Lynne in some damp overcrowded care home with your only source of entertainment is Bingo. Please shoot me now if that is my future – I don't mind being on my own; I don't mind being poor but please save me from Vera Lynn and Bingo.

To sum up me. I am complicated like most people. People see me as shallow. I once watched a documentary about Japan, a long time ago. It stated that Japanese men have 3 layers. The outer layer is for work colleagues and business; the 2nd layer is for family and the 3rd layer is the true self – the one you never share with anyone. I keep my true feelings to myself – no one ever knows those apart from me. I can be tough and not afraid of many things even though as a child I had no confidence and I taught myself to be confident and I found that it was better to take risks than to play safe. I have no fear even if I am down to my last penny – I have been in that situation plenty of times. I know my weaknesses and I know my strengths.

Let me tell you a little story. I support Aston Villa (very confusing for Americans because in the rest of the World they actually put foot to football which they don't in America – for the education of Americans – we call it football because the foot is used for contact with the ball. I know it seems so easy to understand but have sympathy for Americans who find the world a confusing place after the collapse of the Soviet Union. For those who don't know Aston Villa is a football (not soccer – I hit children in China who use the word soccer) club based in Birmingham. Birmingham is a city in the middle of England (hence it is in the Midlands) and is known as the 2nd city of the UK. It was the centre of the Industrial Revolution in the history of the UK. When I was a child cars; motorbikes; metal parts and other industry was still based in Birmingham. Every year (to my shock) it is voted to have the worst British accent by people in the UK. Personally I think the Liverpool accent is the worst.

Anyway to get back to my story. One Saturday I went to see Aston Villa play a match in the Premier League. On one side of Villa Park (the stadium) there is a park called Aston Park. It is possible, if you are lucky, to park for free next to the park and then walk over the park to the ground. I was lucky and found a space to park on the side of the road next to the park. A local man came up to me and said that he would make sure my car was OK for £10. I said fine knowing that there was no chance that I was going to pay it. I returned from the game and no sign of him so got in the car and joined the inevitable traffic jam as 35,000 people are trying to leave at the same time. I am sitting in the car and the man comes up to me. He demands his £10 and I tell him to fuck off. He then just stands there. I felt like stopping the car and berating him for not having a plan when someone tells him to fuck off. He just stood there for 5 minutes and then left. I am the sort of person who can tell you yo fuck off even though I have no idea if you are going to attack me.

Another story which will help you understand me. I worked for the Metropolitan Police as an accountant for 13 years. At the end I decided to engineer my retirement. There were 2 main reasons for this – one was austerity in the UK and the other was boredom. The other major reason is that the Met Police was deliberately managing disabled people out of the organisation. I found that disgusting and even more disgusting were managers abdicating responsibility by claiming that the instruction came from the Commissioner of the Metropolitan Police Bernard Hogan-Howe.

I was a pain in the side of the Met Police as they couldn't intimidate me.

Let me tell some ODF the books I like and films and this might give you an insight into my psyche. I like Charles Dickens; Philip K Dick; William Gibson; History of the Russian Revolution; Thomas Hardy books. The films I like are horror; Apocalypse Now; Good Morning Vietnam; V for Vendetta; Bilitis. I am sure a psychologist would have a field day with my choice of books and films.

I hate injustice and will play by the rules (but didn't someone say that rules are advisory for wise men). I must admit I find it difficult to empathise with people and do get impatient with people who cry – my attitude is you either accept what has happened or you adapt and change the environment you are in. I can be a thug I know that. I was one up to about 14 and then decided to change. I was never in trouble with the law but I did find it easier to fight physically than verbally.

I like sometimes to release that thug side of me. It can be cathartic – there is no restraint; you are not bound by rules of normal society and most people are so shocked that an accountant; a person who appears to be laid back, who does not criticise people for their lifestyle can change.

I once went back to school for a reunion and someone said to me that I was a bit frightening as I was unpredictable – not in a bad way just unpredictable.

I think this was a result of my upbringing in the 70s. The 70s were a violent time – people were more likely to fight than to reason. I learned from that. There always seemed to be lots of bullies at school but I maintained my own status as I was big and could lose my temper in a fight. I was friends with both bullies and everyone else. I suppose I was like Switzerland but I was just bigger.

I was big. My parents gave me lots of food. I used to have 5 slices of toast for breakfast; a cooked lunch and then a cooked dinner. However I was very active – I walked to school a lot of time and back again in the evening (it must have been at least 5 miles each way; I played football every day; went cycling every weekend; did 2 paper rounds and played every sport at school.

A story I suppose sums me up. I did a paper round in a rural part of the Midlands. This meant a lot of cycling to cover the paper round. One morning it was the week before Xmas so, I decided, that when I was delivering the newspapers and magazines to knock on everyone's door to remind them it was Xmas. I bet they did not like being woken up at 630am on a freezing cold morning.

Chapter 6 My wife and family

Who are they?

Obviously personality; background and culture gives an insight into how people will behave and react to circumstances.

So I met my future wife, of course, I didn't know it then. She had a sad story like most Thai women. She had divorced her 1st husband and received no support from him. She had 2 daughters and had no means to support – she was also expected to support her parents as her brother was in prison for raping an 8 year old girl. She was expected to look after her children and her parents without any help from anyone. In Thailand there is minimal support for people if you are ill; retired; sick or poor.

I think that is her motivation – money. I have learned a long time ago that having money makes no difference to your life – oh yes it makes it more comfortable to live but makes no difference to you. If you were a shy person when you were poor you will be a shy person when you are rich; if you were depressed when you were poor you will still be depressed when you are rich; if you were a failure when you are poor you will still be a failure when you are rich. I know this as I have been well off financially and poor. I was still the same person. The only difference was that I spent more time ensuring that I was getting the best investment return on the money than just enjoying it.

My wife never sued her 1st husband for financial support even though she was left with 2 children to support and he went off and had another family which he supported. I worked out during this divorce why this happened – he gave her brother a job as a security guard after he came out of prison for raping an 8 year old girl. The only reason the brother (Ampol Tharaso) was released early was because the King on his birthday every year releases prisoners. My wife sacrificed her own and her daughter's financial security for her brother. Her brother has never supported his sister or his parents while he expected his sister, my wife, to not only provide financial support for her own children but also for their parents.

My wife came from a poor family. The family used to own a lot of land. The grandfather had come from China. A lot of people in Northern Thailand have Chinese ancestors as Chiang Mai is close to China. A lot of Chinese used to drive to Chiang Mai but they were coming in old cars and causing a lot of pollution so the Thai government introduced rules which reduced the number of cars to a trickle.

The key to me keeping the main asset (the house in Thailand) has been the large amount of documentary evidence that I kept from 12 years ago. I had the original documents which made all the difference. My wife has tried to claim in sworn statements in both the UK and Thailand that either I forced her to sign the contracts or she did it out of love to give me some security. Both claims are bullshit. She signed them willingly.

When I first met my wife and her family they seemed fine. I had met my wife when she was working as a prostitute in London and the South East of England - mainly London. I went along to a couple of places when she was working. One was in Stratford in East London. Stratford is a poor part of London located in the South East of London. Traditionally a cockney land but like the rest of London has been gentrified and the middle class by people migrating across London to try to find cheaper housing to buy.

When you went inside it looked as though the building is going to collapse. The walls all had cracks in them and I wondered if I might get buried under all the rubble. It didn't help that the house was on a busy road junction and used to shake every time a lorry went past. It was quite busy and I spent 2 hours with my wife. While I was there she had 2 customers. Obviously they were there for sex.

She was working in the sex industry because she needed the money as she was divorced with 2 young daughters and her parents to support in Thailand. In Thailand even though the priority of parents is to educate and support their sons and not daughters they expect the daughters to look after them, I find that strange, If you expect your daughter to look after you wouldn't you want them to have a good job and earn as much as possible.

My wife was born in a small town at the top of a mountain above the city of Chiang Mai. Chiang Mai was the capital of the North of Thailand. She was born into a big family as her mother was one of 8 sisters. They all lived in the same town. Her grandfather was originally from China. Chiang Mai is a popular place for the Chinese to visit and to stay. So my wife is part Chinese in a small way. Her grandfather was in the Thai army.

My wife's family were poor but they did have a farm. My wife's brother was sent to the temple to be a monk at about the age of 8. It is the greatest honour for a family if their son is a monk. Everyone is a Buddhist in Thailand. Wherever you go you will statues and temples. In the smallest village with about 3 houses, there will be a temple. All Thai people give money and/or food to the local temple. They are still very superstitious even the most educated. I was staying with my wife in her town and I suggested we walk to the local bar for a drink and she refused because the ghosts were in the jungle and might catch you!

My wife is very intelligent but is not intelligent when it comes to understanding UK culture, She has made the mistake of believing that I would react like Thai or other Western men. I have a theory that a lot of people in Europe have a fuck you gene. It is a gene that makes us go fuck you I don't care what the cost is. I think that I have a bigger fuck you gene than most people. We have demonstrated this gene throughout the history of Europe.

My wife is taller than most women in Thailand and taller than a lot of Thai men. I have walked with her in Thailand and she is definitely taller than most Thai men. She thinks this is due to her Chinese grandfather. In China, Chinese people thought she was Chinese and would try to have a conversation with her. When my wife did not answer they thought she was stupid or something.

I would describe her as being of average height for women in Europe - about 5 foot 4 inches. That is tall for Thailand. She is very pretty and has a very sexy body. She is not too big and not too small. She has 34D breasts and she weighs about 57 kg. So not fat either. Like all Thai women she wants to weigh less than 50kg, In China, everyone thought she was Chinese - I didn't think that but the Chinese did.

My wife speaks excellent English - I don't think she has had extensive lessons as she went to a school where they didn't have English lessons. Before I met her she was the manager of a branch of a large supermarket chain which was owned at one point by a Dutch company. My wife was the chief liaison when the Dutch visited the store in Chiang Mai. She took them around the bars after work and negotiated with the bar girls the price for various sexual services. Naturally, her English improved, even more, living with me as we used English every day. We used English every day for 12 years.

She was curious about sex too. Before buying the house in Chiang ma we stayed in hotels. We stayed in one hotel which was next to a popular centre for gays. A lot of Thai men and Western men were there every evening – it was very popular. My wife asked me to go and find out what went on inside. So I did as I was curious.

I went inside and at the reception I was given a key for a locker. I went into the changing room and I noticed that the changing room had a glass wall. The man in the bar could see through the glass war to see you getting naked. Reception had given me a towel and that was all you could wear. There were Thai men and western men all naked. Letting it all hang out. So I got into the swing of it. There was a pool and a gym and a bar. There were also rooms upstairs. I went for a swim and there was only 1 other man in the pool with me. He was getting closer and closer so I decided to beat a hasty retreat. I then visited the gym and bar – no one was in the gym. I then noticed lots of men going upstairs to the rooms. I decided to have a look. That was a mistake. In one of the rooms upstairs, there were about 10 men all on one bed having sex both anal sex and oral sex.

I decided to leave at that point. I was not tempted to join in.

Another time my wife wanted to visit a gay bar – there seems to be a theme developing here for my wife! We went on her scooter looking for a gay bar she had heard of in Chiang Mai. She got a bit lost so she is asking people in the street where the gay bar is located – a bit embarrassing for me! Eventually we found it. It was not very busy – just us and another man.

My wife had come up with a cover story. It went like this – we were brother and sister and I was a bit shy so I needed my sister to come along as well. What a silly story. As soon as I walked in a male member of staff joined me at our table. He stayed the whole evening. On stage there were various Thai men available for hire. The staff member asks me if I like any of them and that if I did there were rooms at the back of the bar for short time use. I don't think he meant for just a lie-down or to surf the internet!. I said that I didn't fancy the men as they were a bit skinny for me.

Also he keeps telling me that at 11pm there is a special show on the stage. So my wife and I stay. The special show was a live sex show involving different staff members. Again he asks me if I fancy any of the men – again I say that they are too skinny for my taste. At the end of the show, we left.

My wife I felt at the time was more western in attitude than most Thai women. I assumed that this was due to being exposed to Westerners in her career in Thailand at the big supermarket chain, Tops and being in the West and dealing with Western men in her job as a prostitute. Also in her job as

Page 115

a Thai masseur, after our marriage, she was talking to English people every day. It is interesting that her friend Vantanee Gresophon in a sworn statement claimed that my wife was not very good at understanding English. Of course, this witness also lied about my wife living with her as all my wife's tax records and credit agency records claim she lives elsewhere. Interesting!

I think it is true after reading about the experience of other men in divorce from Thai women and my experience that Thai women revert to the Thai view of life.

What is that Thai view? It does not matter if you lie about someone and threaten them when it comes to money. That is how my wife has behaved. Theft is alright. What it proves that Buddhism like all religions enables its supporters to behave in any way they please. Lie; steal; threaten people; lie about people – it is OK the God or prophet you worship will always forgive you.

Moving on to the rest of my wife's family. This is made up of her father (her mother died about 5 years ago); her brother Ampol Tharaso and her daughters Lek (real name Vissanee) Laowanit and her other daughter Ploy (real name Kanokporn) Laowanit. I have already mentioned that her brother was a convicted child rapist (raped a girl of 8). They were all from a quite big village called Sameong which is in the mountains above Chiang Mai. Not a very nice family – you have a brother who is a child rapist and you have a mother who wanted my wife to be a prostitute from about the age of 16. The mother wanted her daughter to be a bar girl. In a way you can understand it – the family were and are poor with little education between them.

The Thai people have a complicated view. It appears to the world sometimes that Thai people are a very liberal people – this is not the case. It might seem that they are liberal as there seem to be ladyboys openly living as ladyboys and when you walk down the street there are lots of half-naked Thai women offering all types of sex that you can think of and can't think of! However most Thai people despise ladyboys and bar girls. Ladyboys are treated badly by other Thai people and are restricted as to the type of work they can do. It is very unlikely that a ladyboy would be helped in her village. The same goes for bar girls. The family is happy with the money but no Thai man would want to marry a bar girl. That is why bar girls in Thailand target foreign men.

Thai men have a bad reputation in Thailand. Women see Thai men as children as all the Thai men want to do is gamble; have sex with any women and drink. To a point that is true. Every week in every village in Thailand the men are at the local bar drinking, gambling and trying to have sex with the women in the bar. Up until very recently, it was acceptable for a man to have a wife and a mia noi. A mia noi is literally a little wife. She is looked after by the man who already has a wife but the mia noi does no have any legal rights or recognition. I met this attitude in the Thai court. The court had no problem that I had a girlfriend or what they call a gik but if it was a mia noi then it was a problem. So a man could have a girlfriend – as men have needs. That was the attitude of the court. Very different from most of the rest of the world. What was interesting is that my Thai wife always said I was allowed 3 affairs – clearly not.

My wife's daughters have turned out to be in the same mould of Thai people. They have been prepared to lie and steal from me for money. The eldest daughter Ploy has graduated for lying about a loan I made to her (about £6,000) to help her buy her apartment to stating in a sworn statement that I would force her to come with me to brothels in Chiang Mai for a 3some with her. Amazing after the support I gave her and her family over 10 years when her own father has never given 1 penny in support in 20 years! A warning to any man or woman out there – watch out for Kanokporn Laowanit who works at Bangkok Bank in Chiang Mai.

My wife's daughters are unusual in that Ploy is bisexual and the younger daughter Lek is a lesbian. This upsets my wife as she has the traditional view of sex and does not like that they are not straight. What is amazing is that I don't care and yet my wife and her employer John Hatfield have attempted to besmirch my name by saying that I was obsessed with them in a sexual way. I know that my conscience is clear – I treated my wife's daughters as I would my own. It is ironic that men including a Pete Griffiths who I worked in China many times tried to suggest that I should try something – that horrified me as I saw them as daughters.

My wife and her daughters know that I treated them like family and the claims they make are lies and without foundation but for money, they will say anything.

What is interesting is that all over South East Asia everyone wants to be white. I also point out to people that it is not a good thing to be white in sunny countries as I burn badly if I stay too long in the sun which means that I have to wear long-sleeved T-shirts; stay in the shade and use Factor 50

sunscreen. If I don't then I end up shedding skin in bed as I

have burnt. Not pleasant!

Chapter 7 So how did we get here?

I think that we got where we are – my wife stealing 2 houses and a car from me(and other things) and making all sorts of sexual allegations - because I was too nice. I was supportive financially; emotionally and practically. I think they saw that as a weakness. They are now finding out that I am weak – do you know anyone who would stand up in Thai court and refuse to pay bail knowing that they could go to prison! The one thing I have is big balls!

I met my Thai wife 14 years ago when she was working as a prostitute in London. I met her at a flat in West London. My 1st wife and I were not getting on and the marriage was inevitably heading down the tubes. One of the problems with my 1st wife is that she didn't like sex but she felt obliged to give me sex as she was a wife. She was only interested in 1 position and was not interested in any of my needs and suffered from the only child syndrome – so truly fucked up.

I have found over the years that an only child is really fucked up. My theory is that an only child never has to share; never has to compete; never has to amuse themselves and never learns how to negotiate. They are the centre of the parent's world as the parents are too scared that they will lose their only child both in terms of an accident and in terms of emotional withdrawal from them. Therefore the parents do not want to upset their only child. If you have more than 1 child it is impossible to focus on 1 child as the others will complain and be a pain. Parents should never be allowed 1 child.

You see it in China when you are teaching. China had a 1 child policy. I can understand the policy in some ways – can you imagine what the population of China would be if there had not been a 1 child policy! I see it all the time in China – it is called the Little Emperor syndrome in China. The children are so used to no one saying no to them and parents becoming richer that they have become unpleasant little shits some of them. They believe that because they are the centre of their parents' and grandparent's world that this will continue when they are working. They are in for a rude awakening. Also at some point, China will have a property crash – it is inevitable as property prices are soaring and they are many developments. China is dependent on high economic growth and at some point like Japan China will have a property crash because Chinese banks like banks in Japan before the great crash in Japan are hiding bad loans linked to property values. It is as inevitable as the sun setting. Chinese people must be buying expensive things on credit as they don't earn enough to pay for them.

An example is the teachers I work with in China. I work with teachers who earn 7,000 RMB per month – that is about £800 per month. They have a new car; they have a new apartment; they pay for extra tuition for their children and they buy designer gear form the West. That is not possible on about £800. I earn 15,000rmb – I am lucky as I have a rent-free apartment; I don't pay utilities and I could eat for free all meals at the school for 5 days of the week. I don't have major coats. I will admit that things are cheap in China compared to London in the UK but then London is one of the most expensive cities in the world.

The woman I met (my future wife) was described to me on the phone as being early 30's but in reality was in her 40's though you wouldn't know – it is amazing that Asian women seem to stay longer looking youthful to the Westerner. She was based in a small house in Hanwell in West London usually with another girl being available. She would wear very sexy clothes – most men's dream of what women should wear in bed. She offered me most things – a 3some with the other girl working there; anal sex; or just sex. She was very good at massage as she was Thai. I don't know what it is about Thai women but all of them seem to know how to do Thai massage. It was my 1st experience of sex with a Thai woman or any Asian woman. Naturally I found her attractive.

I kept visiting her while my marriage went down the drain. At one point I met her at a hotel in Kings Cross and she bought another Thai woman with her for a 3some. I have to say that was a good night. She was very good at her job – she was very attentive and spoke very good English.

Thai women are very attractive as they do look after men. I am not a fully modern man – I have no problem with women being in charge at work; I believe that all jobs can be done by men and women and I have promoted and worked with women who are better than me and that does not threaten me as I Know that I am good. I like to play a game with people – which Bond theme best fits you. For me, it is the theme from the Spy Who Loved Me – listen to the lyrics you might be able to work it out.

We were in daily contact and after a couple of months things began to change and I eventually asked her to have lunch with me. I met her at her work in the late afternoon and went to a local restaurant. After that, I began to visit her at her flat in Wood green and began to stay with her when she had a day off. I used to stay overnight. I had no problem with her work. I accepted the realities that Thai women who had no qualifications and came from poor backgrounds had limited options to make money.

I would go straight from work. My work operated a flexi system so I could leave at 4pm in the afternoon. I worked for the Metropolitan Police as an accountant in the central accounting function. This was interesting as you could see how every part of the organisation worked – even the secret undercover and counter-terrorism work. The Met Police needed accountants in order to apply the proper accounting principles to record the income and expense in the correct way in the accounts. I was also a Trade Union rep and Chair of the local branch. If I had not been involved in the Trade Union I think I would have killed someone. It is very difficult to explain how mind-numbingly boring the work could be. They had reduced accountancy work to that of working on an assembly line. If I had wanted to do that I would have worked for British Leyland when I first left school. That was the biggest employer where I lived in the Midlands and my parents expected me to go there. Thankfully I decided otherwise.

The Met Police recruited accountants as in one famous year they relied on Police Officers and unqualified staff to make financial forecasts. These forecasts claimed that the Met Police was going to run out of money. Unfortunately, they discovered later that the forecasts were total nonsense. The Met Police realised it needed financial people that could have a proper system for forecasting. Unfortunately, the Met Police is now going backward with regard to financial controls. I have to say that if you are a Police Officer you can ignore the financial rules in the Met Police. There are lots of examples where Police Officers have stolen money and no action taken against the Police Officers. The controls are there but they are not enforced. The main reason for this is the Met Police is run like little clubs in each department with the biggest club being Police Officers supported by all the little clubs.

I tend to take the view that Grouch Marx stated – I don't want to be a member of any club that would have me as a member. I quickly worked out that in every department in the Met Police there was a ruling clique and that would have bored me. The cliques guaranteed promotion to even the most unqualified person regardless of ability and intelligence. As I was bored and fairly intelligent and bolshie the Trade Union was a good home for me. I could argue with anyone and at any time. I eventually was elected president of the Union in the Met Police just before I left.

My skills were quite useful for the Trade Union as I have always been good at understanding systems and rules even though I treat them as being advisory rather than compulsory. I was a thorn in the side of the Met Police for most of my time there. The problem for the Met Police is what do you do with someone who laughs when they attempt to fire him because of so-called Gross Misconduct. I always told them that I didn't care that they could fire me as I would get a better job outside the Met Police with my skills and experience. I only joined the Met Police at the age of 40 for the pension and that was the only reason and I left because of the changes to the pension – more expensive and less pension.

When I went to her room in a house in Wood Green I would usually turn up earlier than her. All of the people in the house were from Thailand and nearly 80 % of them worked as prostitutes and I would talk to them. I found out a number of things – the cost of all sexual services in London; how the industry worked and how much they paid to obtain a false visa from the British Government through the visa process at the British Embassy in Bangkok, Thailand.

Most of the women from Thailand had paid an agent in Thailand £26,000 to get a fake passport and a UK visa. The passport was normally Chinese. My experience of the visa process in Thailand through an agent suggests that they paid staff at the British Embassy as they gave guarantees that they would get the visa for you. If you did it yourself it was every difficult to get a visa as my experience shows. The women did not have the £26,000 so they paid it off from their earnings in the UK from prostitution. I attended a few parties where Thai women were celebrating paying off the money. I didn't know what happened to my wife's debt after she was deported.

The price then for various services were pretty uniform – they did not vary much in the market they were engaged in. I think it would be fair to say for the economists out there that the market for sexual services was a very good example of a perfect competition market – lots of buyers and sellers and not one buyer or seller can control the price in the market. Obviously, if you cater to much richer clientèle then you can charge more.

I learned that prices started at £50 and went up. The £50 was for a basic service of 1 girl and it was 1 service. The one service could be oral sex; anal sex or a handjob. It was supposed to be for 30 minutes but most men could never survive the full 30 minutes and it was usually over in about 5 minutes. If a sexy woman is giving you a blow job you will not last very long – every man knows that. If you wanted 2 girls it was £80 (discount for 2 girls). The girls did not touch each other – if you wanted that you paid more.

I heard a lot of stories about what men would pay for. Men paying to be kicked in the balls for 30 minutes or men paying to be watching eating a flake with the girl's shit out of a plastic bag or put clamps on the man's nipples. They also seemed to go with much older men. Most of them would service men over 60. They were very popular and in demand as they were all Thai and this is a type of woman that is in demand in the sex industry in the UK. I don't know what the attraction is of Thai women but I think I can guess.

They are very pleasant to men they look good and have a gorgeous body. They are all good at massage. Perhaps you can take the girl out of prostitution but you can't take the prostitute out of the girl!

As I said my future Thai wife started to invite me to her flat in Wood Green and I would stay the night. It was every Wednesday. You have to remember I was still married to an English woman. The excuse I gave my wife was that I was playing table tennis away from home with the Met Police table tennis club. I don't know if she really believed me. The Thai girl I was getting more involved with whose English name was Nicky would cook for me or get some food in. I would stay the night and she would give me great blow jobs and great sex.

Nicky worked all over London in different flats and even worked in Worthing, Sussex which was a long way from London. I never asked her how she chose which places she chose to go to and work. I did visit a couple such as the one in Hanwell, West London – which was not very far from my home – and Stratford in East London once. She did wear some very sexy lingerie and she was very popular with clients. I think she also worked in Finchley, North London but I never visited that one as I was still married and had to juggle work; wife; family and girlfriend. It can get complicated and men are not very good at remembering all the various names; birthdays etc.

So I would visit her at a couple of brothels in London. While I was there she would go and service clients. This did not cause me any concerns or disgust me in any way. I am very liberal and understand that people do all sorts of different things and enjoy all sorts of different things. I have tended to the view that if he doesn't hurt anyone and the person involved is able to take part freely or not then it is up to them what they do. It might seem surprising considering that I had a typical working-class upbringing near Birmingham.

My family was very working class. Before I was 7 my family suffered the usual instability of most working-class families of having somewhere to live. I can remember lots of homes before the age of 7. But that has not made me paranoid about money or having somewhere to live. All it has done has made me never want to stay in a caravan ever again – even for a holiday.

The reason for my hating caravans is that we lived in one as a family from when I was 5 to the age of 7. It was in a small village in the Midlands in the middle of nowhere. It was not a very big caravan but it did have one advantage and that it was in the middle of the countryside – one big playground for me. However the caravan had no toilet and no bathroom. It had gas lights and we used a car battery for the TV which meant that you could only watch TV for an hour or 2 in the evenings. For warmth in Winter there was a wood stove – in Winter when you wake up in the morning it is fucking freezing – fucking is the right word for it.

I did not like the village we were in because I had to go to school. I did not want to go to school and my stubborn streak came out very early. In assembly one morning – in the 60s and 70s every school had morning assembly where you said the Lord's Prayer and you sand hymns – even today I remember the hymns but the religion I have left well behind. One morning we were sitting down at assembly on the floor and I just pissed on the floor – just to show my displeasure at being there. As the pee travelled all over the surrounding area the other kids quickly made a big circle around me. At one time I was also locked in the cloakroom – I don't remember what that was for but managed to escape. I was reminded of the escape from school by someone at high school about 9 years later.

I also at 6 at Primary School refused to eat my pudding at lunch. For some reason, the teachers made an issue of it. It might be because every time you didn't finish food at home your mother would say -" Think of the starving children in the world". I never understood how that worked - if I eat all my food they get better. The teachers said to me that if I didn't eat it hen I would sit there all afternoon until I did. I think you can guess what happened - I refused to eat it all afternoon from about 12.30 to 4pm. I thought it tasted disgusting so I wasn't going to eat it. I am still the same - if I think I am doing something right or won't accept your view then I am prepared to be stubborn.

I had a lot of fights at school as the school I went to was very tough. A sort of initiation ceremony at my school was to push a 1st year down the stairs at break time. This was high school. The high school I was at had an annexe which had 5 floors of stairs so it was perfect if you saw a 1st year walking down the stairs was to give them a nudge. My experience in life has made me very tough. I appear laid back to everyone but I am very tough underneath. If you do upset me then allied with my physical size I will go all out to teach you a lesson either through my intelligence or through my physical side. A few people have found that out - not many but a few. If I lose then I always have a plan B. I always say to people you should always have a plan for life; for a situation for anything. If you have a plan then you know what steps to take to achieve that plan and what to do if the plan doesn't work (Plan B).

I am astounded by the number of people in the UK who have no plan as to where they want to be in 5, 10 or 20 years. My brother is a good example. He has no plan for his retirement. He has no hobbies so what is he going to do when he is no longer working? How is he going to pay for retirement? What is he going to do with the time? My brother has no interest in sport; he does not support any football tea; he has no hobbies and he has no interests. I always say to people that people's interests and hobbies make them interesting. I don't care what the hobby - it can be the history of fly fishing from 192 to 1925 for all I care but at least you have something to talk about. What do you talk about if someone has no interests and no hobbies in life - particularly a man.

I could not live with my brother. I have this dream or nightmare that his wife will die before him and out of sympathy as he has no money and no life I will offer to let him stay with me in Thailand. It would be like the Odd Couple - I would be the Jack Klugman character - drinking; women; parties and he would be the continually disproving character. I reckon I would kill him. I felt the same about my job in the Met Police in London - if I had not been a nuisance doing my Trade Union work I think I would have killed someone out of boredom!

Women I am with always complain that they have never seen me cry. I don't - I don't see the point. It does not solve the problem and I don't see how it helps you. I gave up crying when I was about 12 years old. It had not changed the situation and had done nothing for me. I am tough but it does not mean that I expect other people to be the same. I have noticed that people who come from tough backgrounds and have done well divide into 2 groups. The 1st group attributes everything they have done to themselves and does not believe that the Government should give any help to someone who is poor and is living a tough life - after all they did it why can't everyone else. The other group I belong to I recognise that without the help of the Government and the help of teachers I would not be where I am today. I try to help everyone and I am very laid back because of where I come from. I have been very poor and I have quite wealthy - in both situations I have been the same. I have always said that if I won the lottery it would not change my lifestyle - the only thing it would do is make travelling easier.

Everyone I work always asks why I am always cheerful. There is a very easy answer. If you come from the background I do and you have a pleasant job and you can buy what you want and do what you want then every day is a bonus. My 1st wife was not like that and nor is my brother. For them life is a daunting prospect; a struggle and a period of time to endure. Never to enjoy because there will always be something that will spoil the good times. I can't live like that.

Let me explain. I don't like cars - to me they are a box on 4 wheels. So I don't drool over a Ferrari or a Lotus. I don't find gold Apple phones exciting. I see people's love for Apple like a religious cult. Everything Steve Jobs said to the followers of the religion of Apple was like God speaking - spending £1,000 on a mobile phone makes no sense to me. Clothes do not interest me. I don't change my underpants until there are holes in them. The only things I would spend money on are motorbikes and travel. I would travel 1st class everywhere and buy motorbikes.

Motorbikes are my 1st love. I have taught myself to do most things on a motorbike. I can service and sort out the electrics. I can even take apart a motorcycle engine and put it back together. The only thing I miss about the UK is servicing my own motorbikes. I go into a Zen moment when I m working on a motorcycle. A good example is I spent 4 hours working on a motorbike in the UK and I thought only 30 minutes had gone by. I was in that zone. The reason I don't service my motorbike in Thailand is that servicing is so cheap in Thailand and it is difficult to buy the oil etc. But when I finally retire I will service my motorbike. I will have the time to do it.

At that age of 6 I was independent and my parents used the time-honoured method adopted by working-class parents of neglect to make me independent and get on with life. I walked to and from school every day on my own and this was using the local roads and there was some traffic – clearly I did not die from neglect. I used a similar method with my sons – even though people I knew thought I was committing some sort of child abuse.

From the age of 7 we lived in a council house which made a big difference as it was a new house and was in a small town. I don't remember all the moves we made as a child but I don't remember it causing me any problems. In fact, I think it has made me stronger emotionally about change and more flexible about things that happen in my life.

This background has probably made me more accepting and less critical of people's lifestyles and attitudes as I have seen many people when I was a child being bigoted and having closed minds. The working class of my childhood had no interest in the world and had a childish patriotism that meant that they just hated other nations and peoples but could not articulate why they did. It was something vague like they were foreign. My parents still call Black people "coloured". It sounds just like something from Apartheid South Africa.

I believe that I was lucky that I was going to school in the 70s. The teachers teaching then had more freedom in what they taught in the classroom. I first started to love Classical music and Shakespeare because sometimes in Rural Studies lessons a teacher would play Mozart or we would read a Shakespeare play like Twelve Night (this still remains my favourite play).

My laid back view of what my future wife was dong probably comes from that background. I also learned from the maid how the economics of prostitution works with regard to the premises they use. The maid was an interesting character. She was a black woman from the West Indies and had done the same job since she came to the UK. Her job as the maid was to answer the phone; keep the place clean; account for the money taken and generally support the girls and also look after the owner of the flat. I used to talk to her a lot when Nicky was occupied with a client. The maid was a good person. She helped a lot of girls or tried to help them by giving them extra money from the takings of the brothels or helping them to find a doctor etc. She has dome great stories about the daughters of famous people who worked as prostitutes.

The UK has a lot of hypocrisy when it comes to prostitution and drugs. The lawmakers of the UK always condemn both but we all know that at some point they have indulged in either one of them or both. Particularly lawmakers who are in their 50s or 60s as they were part of the generation that went to University and did not need to worry about student debt or jobs or AIDS. Drugs; sex and Rock 'n' Roll were freely available at University and there were no worries about debt or AIDS. At University I never slept in my own bed – I was either in my bed with a girl or in the girl's bed. Also men at University did not need to worry about a rape allegation if they woke up with a girl who had been drunk the night before. If a girl told you she was pregnant you basically told her to fuck off as there was no DNA testing either – you assumed the girl was on the pill when you fucked her. So I find it amazing when lawmakers talk about drugs and how bad they are when they were probably high as kites for most of their 3 years at University.

The maid had an interesting life – a poor and a hard life at times. In some ways, we were similar and got on well. She has told me a lot of stories about her life as a maid in various brothels across London. The girls and how some of them are treated very badly and sometimes how she has worked with the daughters of famous men. I never did ask if the men who were famous knew their daughters were working as prostitutes. The men who paid the girls for sex did not realise the girls had famous fathers.

The maid had met Nicky in the UK when they were working together in brothels in London. So the maid knew Nicky before I met Nicky. They were friends as they stayed at each other's homes and worked together for about 10 hours or more a day. So the maid has known Nicky for nearly 12 years and I have been lucky that she has not been prepared to support Nicky in her allegations and claims about me. It is interesting that women have not believed Nicky in her claims about me while men have been prepared to do so. The women have known me very well and observed my behaviour and my support for my stepdaughters. The women who have lived with us and seen us on a regular basis have taken the view that I have been good to my wife and her family.

The maid came from the West Indies a long time ago with a child. She had left her husband as he was abusive towards her. She would surely see if a man was abusive or see the signs of an abusive man. She had no money when she came and was offered a job as a maid. Not a maid in a hotel but a maid in a brothel. A maid in a brothel is someone who answers the phone; looks after the girls; makes sure the room is kept clean and manages the money collected from customers. The finances of a brothel are quite interesting. If you pay £50 then the maid gets £10 and the escort gets £20 to £25 as the owner of the property gets his/her share. Even though it does not seem a lot for the girl (£20) some girls can make extra money by seeing clients outside the brothel as they keep all the money. There is no tax to pay and if they are in a good area they can make £100 to £200 per day in cash. That is about £1,000 to £1,200 per week or more which equivalent to a gross salary of £95,000 if you were paying tax. A very good wage. This explains how it can be very lucrative and worth women paying to obtain a false passport in an Asian country.

One night I received a message that Nicky (my future wife) had been arrested. I received the message on my mobile as I had been on a course as I was taking a MPA (Masters of Public Administration) degree. The message was from one of the Thai women I had met in the Wood Green house. They informed me that Nicky had been arrested by UK Immigration while working at a flat in Worthing in Sussex. It was 9pm so there was nothing I could do. I phoned them back and found out where she was being held.

The next day I took the day off work saying that I had a family problem and had to sort it out. I have to say that working for the Met Police at that time was good as the organisation was trying to change and had introduced more employee-friendly policies and was trying to change the culture of the Met Police. Ultimately it was too fail as the

Commissioner jumped into too quickly to defend Police Officers without finding out the true story as to what had happened. The culture of the police was too ingrained in him. After that with austerity and a new Commissioner who was definitely a Commissioner who would defend and support whatever Police Officers did the changes were doomed to failure. A pity as if the changes had been carried on the Met Police would be a much better organisation and would have rooted out the racist and sexist culture.

I found out where Nicky was and phoned the Immigration centre she was being held. I had a bit of a problem in that I wasn't sure about her real name as she was using 2 passports – one was Chinese and the other Thai. However, I managed to speak to her not for very long but at least it was contact. I had decided I was going to leave my wife a long time ago. We had married for 20 years and I had come to the point when I had had enough.

I had been very patient. On every holiday my wife bought her parents. Every Easter; every Xmas; every summer my wife brought her parents on holiday with us. Even though they only lived less than a mile from us her parents came to stay with us at Xmas for at least 2 weeks.

It was very weird. The only explanation I think of is that her parents were 40+ when she was born. She was an only child and I have come to the conclusion that no one should have only 1 child. Only children are fucked up because they never have to compete with a sibling; never have to share; and are never alone as their parents concentrate on amusing the child 100% of the time. The child also feels they have to repay this back to their parents.

Eventually, I got fed up with this. I did suggest compromises but that was not possible. So, in the end, I just gave up. I just went along and I would go off on my own for some fun. The worst part was that I was the tour manager; the ticket agent and the entertainer for my wife and her family. My wife would demand I talk to her when I was looking forward to sitting by the pool and relaxing. Her favourite phrase on holiday was we can't waste time. Do you know if I want to waste fucking time on holiday I can and I will!

So my future wife was locked up but I hadn't decided at that point to marry her. I did like her a lot as she was everything my wife wasn't. I had decided to leave my wife but I was waiting until the children were older. They were 15 and 12 at that point. I had 2 sons and I was going to wait until they left school but being with the Thai woman was nice and made me realise what I was missing and that I couldn't wait another 4 or 5 years. I decided to leave my wife early.

I had just found out that Nicky was being held at the Immigration centre. We talked briefly. I went to a lawyer in Ealing West London. This was 2003. I had told my wife that I wanted a divorce. I was surprised she was upset as we had not been getting on for 4 years at that point. Her parents were no longer involved in our life as they had died. I had arranged a flat to stay in so that I could move out of the family home. Thank God they had died.

They were not adults as they contributed to the break up of our marriage. It is impossible to believe that they thought that any marriage could survive their intervention and blackmail. Yes, blackmail. They once said – if we don't go on holiday with you we can't go anywhere. It is interesting that they managed to go on a cruise; a trip to South Africa and a lot of trips all over Europe and the UK. Yet every time I had any holiday they had to be on holiday with us. I even decided to take my golf clubs to Florida so I could get some time on my own.

Even their prejudices were transferred to my wife. We never bought a Ford car or an automatic as her parents didn't like them or they considered them unreliable. The routes we took to places in the UK was dictated by their view of the trip. I once made a decision of my own to use the M1 to go to Yorkshire and my wife went ballistic – it was like I had just killed her favourite pet in front of her or had shot her parents in the head. It was just amazing.

The trips to Yorkshire were a nightmare. Naturally the parents had to come with – all in one car. 4 adults and 2 children along with all the luggage for a week! What a fucking holiday. We started off staying at her Aunt's in Scarborough – I did that a couple of times and then no more. I didn't know what was going on but the Aunt had strict rules – in bed before 10pm and no use of any appliances and no heating allowed. I think prison would have been more comfortable! During the day we all went to a hut on the beach front facing the North Sea with the cold wind whistling off it.

Some of you won't know Scarborough. It is a genteel traditional seaside resort full of cafés; cheap restaurants and strange people who have weird accents. This is not the place to go if you are gay. They probably still had the stocks for people who read the Guardian or liked to go to the theatre –

witchcraft! The North Sea is one of the most unpleasant seas in the world but it has fish and oil in it. Every day in Scarborough was cold on that beachfront. We played cards all day; ate cold sandwiches; huddled around this small gas hob when the kettle was on and were not allowed to do anything interesting or enjoyable. They had done this every year for about 30 years. The comment of my future mother in law was that it was only once a year. You think I am going to waste my free time on this crappy town in the North of England when there was a warm sunny world out there.

This reminds me of my brother. I think it is a working class thing. When I was a child my grandparents always went to the same place every year for a holiday. They went to Rhyll in Wales. We did the same when I was a child. I have to say that it used to take us ages to get anywhere. I am sure that my father drove at about 40 miles per hour – even on the motorway. At the age of 9 I thought this was slow. I think I realised this as every other car went past us on the road.

My brother carried on the tradition of going to the same place for 20 years. He and his family went camping in Weymouth for 20 plus years. Weymouth is quite nice as at least it is warm and sunny but a tent at the age of 50 plus. I have reached the age now when I like my creature comforts – I like a proper bed at night; I like my bathroom a short walk away; I like the English Breakfast in the morning; the cup of tea in bed; watching the evening programmes on TV and being able to leave my stuff in a locked room.

What holiday have you got in a tent? A walk across a windy field to the toilet; wind blowing through the tent at night; an uncomfortable bed; no en-suite bathroom with a nice shower. My brother is strange but I think he is just a product of his environment – a product of a home life as a child that was not the best. H is so slow at doing anything. I went skiing with him as I bought him a skiing trip for his 40th birthday. He was so slow at getting ready in the morning as we shared a room.

We arrived before him – myself; my wife; a friend and the dog. We had the tent up quite quickly as we followed the instructions. My brother and his family finally arrived. He has a wife and 2 daughters. At that time his daughters were about 16. His wife must be one of the ugliest women on the planet and one of the laziest. When I took a year off after retiring in 2015 I used to phone her during the day. It was amazing. She always used to say that she was exhausted. I used to ask her why and the reason was that usually she had been looking after a child for 2 hours! All of 2 hours – in London people commute more than 2 hours and still do a day's work. I always imagined her as a middle-class Victorian woman who had never worked and had maids to look after her. I could imagine her lying down on a chaise longue fanning herself as she had the "vapours". They were made for each other. She had every allergy you could think of in the world – she was lactose intolerant; gluten; and everything else. But she was never tested. Their daughters also had the same problems. The food they cooked without gluten and milk tasted horrible. I used to suggest to my brother we go shopping to get proper food. He loved the food we bought – proper chocolate biscuits; proper chocolate etc. I used to say to him why he didn't buy them and he used to say he wasn't allowed!

When I went skiing with him in France we arrived about 6pm from Geneva by car. That night we had to go to a restaurant for a meal as the chalet girls had the night off. We hired everything – skis; pass and boots then went for dinner. At the restaurant my brother was looking at the menu and I asked him what he was going to have. He responded in his usual way – slowly. He stated that he wanted the lasagne but he wasn't allowed to by his wife. This astounded me. I said that I would not tell his wife as long as he didn't! So he had lasagne! The reason he wasn't allowed lasagne along with any beef products was because of mad cow disease. My view was that most of us could have been eating contaminated beef for years so it was too late now – anyway I like my meat too much!

Prior to breakfast we were up at the same time. As I was dressed and my brother was more than half-dressed I said to my brother that I was going to breakfast and that I would see him there. I thought he would be about 10 or 15 minutes – 45 minutes he appeared. It was worse than a woman. As a female friend said men are lucky as they are wash and go! This sums him up he is strange. There are a few other things I just don't get – he won't answer the phone on a Saturday because it might be telesales and if he does answer the phone he doesn't say anything in case it is an automated telesales call. He also hardly ever answers the phone when he is at home as his wife does.

Back to the wonderful camping trip. My brother and his family arrived. They have for nearly 20 years been putting up the same tent. They took about 2 hours to put this tent up. My brother did everything – he cooked breakfast for them;

washed up; did the shopping and made the tea in the morning. He was very jealous because I did not cook or wash up. He actually asked me if I did anything and I said you need to play to your strengths and cooking is not one of mine. I suggested we go for a proper breakfast as, after all, this is the seaside and there must be a café which does an English breakfast by the seaside – it is a seaside institution in the UK. We found one and my brother's family are very fussy. In the evening we went to the port and bought fish and chips but we had to go to a particular shop as they were the only one to sell gluten free fish and chips – not recommended as far as I can taste! What was amazing I knew more about Weymouth than he did even though it was mu 1st trip to the town and his 20th!

The best view I have ever heard was expressed by my brother's wife when she stated that riding a motorbike around Bromsgrove was more dangerous than London! I couldn't be bothered to argue even though Bromsgrove is a small market town where nothing happens. Although I did read on the

Internet that you can now buy customised sex dolls from a company in Bromsgrove. Bromsgrove has arrived!

Everybody who knows myself and my money always asks the same question – are you sure you are from the same family? Were you adopted? Were you found on the doorstep? Even my brother's daughters asked the same question. Horrors of horrors one day my brother's youngest daughter turned to my brother and asked why Daddy couldn't be more like Uncle John. I though don't say that! I am different and you have to ask how does that happen. My brother had the same parents; lived in the same house; went to the same school; had the same teachers yet I am totally different from him in outlook; attitude and personality. I like to take risks; I like to just provoke people to get a reaction and I have an enhanced feeling about justice. I am not afraid to say something if I think it is wrong.

From an early age I lost any faith in a supernatural all-powerful God. I remember from the age of 11 I would question the teachers as to why we were going to Church at Easter and I also had a long argument once with a man who was invited to preach to us in the Cub scouts. I think I am not good with being told what to do. I think I follow the view that rules are advisory for wise men! It is a good thing that National Service was abolished before I had to do it because I would have been terrible in the Army or Air Force or Navy. I can imagine me filling a Tank with jam to see how much jam it would take.

I have been lucky as I have never really been punished for my behaviour. I think people see that my behaviour is not malicious and is usually quite funny as I take the piss out of officialdom. However, the Met Police did try to sack me at least once a year over a period of 12 years. People in the Met Police used to say to me that they knew when I was bored as I would send out an email to me Trade Union officials in the Met Police winding them up. At times it was very easy. Perhaps not being afraid in the Met Police of being sacked helped me to say to the court in Thailand that I was refusing to pay bail.

Also, the times I was brought up in I think helped in terms of my ability to say No and not to be concerned about the possible consequences. I was brought up in the 60s and 70s when everything was changing. Schools were at the forefront of the changes in attitudes. School teachers shared my background as they were post-war and had been teenagers in the 60s. The racism that had been so casual and sexism and inequality were all being challenged along with International campaigns against Apartheid and the situation in Rhodesia (now Zimbabwe). My parents still refer to "coloured people". I also remember the adverts in local shop windows advertising rooms where it stated that "Coloured people, Irish and dogs were not allowed". As a child I found it perplexing.

I was always left to my own devices by my parents. They never attended parent's evenings and did not give any advice as to what options I should choose for 'O' levels (GCSE now) or provide any support when I went to the dentist or eye checks or anything. I sorted out everything myself from about the age of 11. I had a great deal of freedom and it is amazing how without any advice; guidance or support how I made my way through life as a child. They didn't even read school reports. I think nowadays someone from Social Services would be investigating. But this was the 1970s and society tended to believe in neglect being the way for children to find their place in the world. I certainly remember that all my friends were kicked out of the house during holidays so that they wouldn't mope at home or get in the way. Most of us went out in the morning and only came back for food when hungry and only went back home when it was dark – which in the summer could be quite late.

I don't think my parents understood the modern world as it was changing. It was changing too fast. The profession I was in sums up the changes in society. I was an accountant from the 1980s and accountancy changed beyond all recognition.

From the 2nd World War accounting offices used to be manual ledgers and manual invoicing and manual reconciliations. It had not changed since the Victorian period. Then in the 60s computers started to come in and computers took over the manual side of the profession. Accountancy changed from a boring manual type of labour to a more advisory and consultancy role and became more involved in the processes of the organisation. The accountancy profession is now totally different.

My parents' life had not really changed for them for decades. You went to work in a factory; you worked hard and you got paid every week in cash. You could get a Government house which was quite cheap to rent life wasn't easy but you could manage and it didn't vary. They would also go to the local Working Men's Club for entertainment. You can see this life in countless films made in the '60s. Then society started to change and left them behind. They couldn't understand why I didn't want to work in a factory making cars. I had more ambition and this was difficult as the working class didn't have ambition.

The expansion of Universities and the financial support of the UK Government's changed all this. I could go to University as the Government paid my tuition fees and gave me money to live on each year. Also as only about 12% of students went to University there were plenty of jobs paying very well. Companies used to come to University each year to attract students to work for them – it was called the Milk Round. In my opinion it was the greatest betrayal of working-class kids when the Labour Party from 1997 wanted 50% of students to go to University. It wrecked that chances of the working class advancing in the UK. This is shown in the statistics of unemployed or underemployed graduates from working-class backgrounds. The rich and Middle Classes have contacts and more highly regarded schools to get them good graduate jobs. North Bromsgrove High School doesn't have the same kudos as Eton when it comes to getting a job as a graduate! Nor does Essex University have the same kudos as Edinburgh! What benefited the bright working-class kid was the money to stop the pressure in poor families to work – that is the main problem for working-class kids. If you are living in poverty you will not go to University if you have to pay for it with loans.

I had a lot of pressure put on me to work at British Leyland when I was 16. They did not want me to take 'A' levels –they wanted me to work. British Leyland was the forerunner to Rover and was the biggest employer for people where we lived. A lot of stories have been told about work practices at British Leyland (BL) in the 70s. People sleeping during the night shift and people clocking for other people who were working at another company at the time. Also, most people took parts from work (for free) for their own cars. My father always knew someone in the body shop at BL who would repair the car or provide a part for the car. My stubborn streak came out and I made sure that I did my 'A@ levels.

I always remember career advice at school. It was woeful.
There were low expectations for working-class students at
school There was no imagination. If you were a working-
class kid there were some jobs that were considered
impossible for you – like Investment banking; research;
Directors of large companies. I think they worked to a simple
formula – if you were good at Maths then joining a Bank was
a good idea; if you were an intelligent girl then secretarial
work was good for you and if you were considered stupid
then a building site or British Leyland was your career advice.
It was woeful! When you were 15 or 16 it was compulsory to
see Careers Advice – what a waste of time.

Life was different when I was a teenager. Anyway back to my
story of what happened in my marriage and how we got to a
situation where I have people attacking me; my wife stealing
assets from me and how I am winning. It might not seem like
winning but it is and I am going to keep the house.

As I said we met in the UK. My future wife was a prostitute working in various brothels across London and the South East. I was working for the Metropolitan Police as an accountant and I was also a Trade Union official. I was a rep and Chair of the local Branch in the Met Police. I was unusual as a rep as I was educated; a senior manager in the organisation and had not spent my life in the Met Police. Most staff in the organisation had been there from the age of 18 and when I arrived they were still there after 30 or 35 years. I quickly realised that in the Police Staff part of the Met Police each department was managed by a ruling clique and I tend to take the view of Grouch Marx that I did not want to be a member of a club that would have me!

The job was boring but I only joined for the pension at the age of 40. If I had not joined the Union and decided to be difficult I think that I might have killed people out of sheer boredom - particularly towards the end. People used to say that they knew I was bored as I would send out a controversial email to everyone that upset some elected officials or upset the Met Police or upset some members. I like it when I am bored to throw a rock into the puddle - just to see what would happen. I think the Met Police tried to get rid of me every year but failed each time. The only reason I became heavily involved with the Union is that I was bored in the Met Police.

The work was boring and I quickly worked out that the only way to get a promotion was to become a "company" man. I saw people get promoted in the Finance Dept in the Met Police even though they didn't have the qualifications. The best example of this was when someone was promoted after a memo had been sent out stating that if you didn't have an accounting qualification then you couldn't be promoted above a certain level. Within months of this one man was promoted to a post that required accountancy qualification when he didn't have any. The Met Police was rife with nepotism. People got promoted because they were good drinkers or they carried the bag of senior managers or they played football with senior managers etc. For Police Officers it was even better they were guaranteed a job (even though it was always officially denied) after they retired or were sick. I once complained to someone in the Finance Dept that Tube fares had gone up again and they stated it didn't affect them as they were a Police Officer. I was astounded as they had been in the Finance Dept as long as me. Even people outside the Met Police knew that retired police officers could move into a police staff role. I tell you the training that Police Officers get for 2 years or less means they can do any job - IT support; accountancy; human resources; property management - amazing this police training isn't it (that is sarcasm by the way).

Eventually, the divorce from my 1st wife comes through and I visit the Thai woman in Thailand and meet her family - 2 daughters and her daughters. We were getting on well while my divorce in the UK was going through. I was still working in the UK so I was very busy at the time. I had moved out of the family home with my 1st wife and was renting a flat not too far away. I did not have a lot of money as the divorce was expensive - legal fees - plus travelling to Thailand. My soon to be wife was trying to make money in Thailand and opened a noodle place in her village. She had given up a very good job with a large supermarket chain in Chaing Mai in the north of Thailand. She was a manager of a branch but had given it up to go to the UK to be a prostitute as this was suggested by her Aunt. Her Aunt had been based in Scotland but in London you could earn more.

I got on well with her family and I decided after doing some research that I could live in Thailand for a number of reasons. The one thing that I hate about the UK is that the weather is too unpredictable - summer can be cold; winter can be warm and you can have snow in April. In Thailand the weather is very predictable - a rainy season or a dry season. Weather forecasts in Thailand are very easy - it just depends on whether you are in the rainy or dry season!

My future wife had to look for more money even though she had a good job that paid well by Thai standards and had good prospects as she never asked for any support from her ex-husband and he never provided any. For a long time I could never work out but during the present divorce I discovered why she never took any action. Her brother (Ampol Tharaso) had been in prison for raping an 8 year old girl when he was young. He was released early on one of the birthday days of the King of Thailand - he released so many prisons every year. Her brother clearly couldn't get a job as he has no qualifications and the prison sentence did not help. Her ex-husband gave her brother a job as a security guard where the ex-husband was a manager. I believe that her brother still works there. In the UK the brother (Ampol Tharaso) would not be allowed to work in a shopping centre in security with lots of families going there. The shopping centre he works at is one of the biggest in Thailand - it is called Futurepark.

My wife has been the only one to support her parents. Her brother has provided no support whatsoever. He was a Buddhist priest from an early age and gained no qualifications from school. He is married but has no children - my wife says that it is a good thing and could be punishment for his behaviour with children in the past. The ex-husband supports his new family as he has children. Not a penny for his 2 daughters.

Finally the UK divorce came through. This meant that I could now restart my life. I had received £350,000 from the divorce and that is the reason that it took so long as it had taken a long time to negotiate. We were actually at Family Court with the judge waiting while the 2 barristers went between the 2 rooms we were in negotiating a settlement. At that point I decided to take 4 months off from work at the Met Police. You didn't get paid but you could return to your old job after the break. The reason for this was for me to spend time in Thailand and see if it was for me long term. I had not spent much time in Thailand - I had visited it on the way to Australia with my old family to visit family in Australia. I had made some short visits to visit the new Thai girlfriend. So this was a sort of fact-finding visit. To check out the cost of living in Thailand; to check out property; to check out the girlfriend and her family and to see more of Thailand.

I quickly that in Chiang Mai that property was quite cheap - you could buy a house for £15,000 and an apartment for about £10,000. From a financial viewpoint having somewhere to live in Thailand would be very cheap. Also there is no council tax; no TV Licence fee; no gas charges (I have not found mains gas anywhere in Thailand); electricity was much cheaper; eating out is much cheaper and having a drink at a bar was much cheaper. The only problem in Thailand is that foreigners are not allowed to own land - which is a bit of a problem as houses are built on land.

However like most countries in Asia, the Thai legal system provides a way for the foreign person's interest in the property to be recognised and registered.

There were lots of properties to choose from in Chiang Mai. Chiang Mai is the main city in the North of Thailand. It is much smaller than Bangkok (the capital) but it still has all the modern amenities like fast internet and cable services etc. The main problem with Chiang Mi is that it does not have a very good taxi service; it has less choice when it comes to shopping and it is more difficult to find someone to do building work or repairs. It also takes more time to get things done. However it is quieter; there are fewer traffic jams and there are fewer people. There is also less pollution apart from the field burning period when there is a lot of burning which creates the worst pollution in Thailand.

Not a bad place to live. So I decided to buy a house in Chiang Mai as I had the money and it meant that there would always be somewhere for me to live when I retire and therefore save money in retirement. I think you could survive on the UK state pension in Chiang Mai if you did not have to pay rent as I would not with a house already paid for. It is quite cheap to get repairs done.

I looked at a number of new developments on the outskirts of Chiang Mai not in the centre as that would be noisy and lots of traffic. I looked at a house that had 6 bedrooms and 6 bathrooms and a garden big enough for parties and it only cost £120,000. Can you imagine how much that would cost in the UK? In London where I am based it would be at least £2m! I decided to go with the smaller house on another development which was a 4 bedroom house with 3 bathrooms and a nice garden. This cost £86,000.

I had the money as I had divorced my 1st wife and worked away with £350,000 in cash. It took time as I have said before but it was worth it. This is the reason I criticise men in the UK and Thailand who just give in and accept that their wife walks away with the assets and the man is left with the debts. There are so many men from and in the UK who are my age who have told me their stories and it is a very familiar story. They end up renting a bedsit and it takes them years to pay off the debts. My view and I express this view very clearly, that it only increases the number of divorces that are not amicable as women tell other women that they can get everything on divorce. The men who just give in make that prophecy true which does not help the rest of us men. Women talk to each other and tell other women divorcing that they can get whatever they want. I have refused to give in and in my 1st divorce walked away with £350,000 and in my Thai divorce I am on my way to getting all the assets in the divorce. I will come back to this later.

While I was in Thailand for 4 months on leave I bought the house and we got married. It is quite cheap to get married. I think the whole wedding including clothes and a party for about 60 people was about £10,000 which was the whole package including photos; flowers; priest; whiskey etc. It would be more expensive now as we were getting nearly 65 Thai baht to the £ now it is 38! Thank you the stupid people of the UK for voting for Brexit - the £ is going down the toilet! Never underestimate the stupidity of the British! Just imagine how the £ will do in the advent of a No Deal Brexit!

While I was on my 4 months break from work in the UK I met an American. He was a stereotypical American - in other words he knew nothing about the country he was living in and understood nothing of the culture. He wanted to stay long term but he had no idea what the rules were in Thailand. I have met so many of them on my travels who are exactly the same. It is very easy to do your research before you arrive in a country - you can even do it while you are in a country. I met him in a coffee shop in one of the shopping malls in Chiang Mai while my wife was shopping.

I have to explain my love for shopping. I hate shopping! All I want to do is go to a shop to know exactly where the stuff I want to buy and leave quickly when it comes to paying. I hate shops that change the layout - I bet they would say it "enhances" customer service - No it is done to make you wander around the store making impulse purchases. It does not work with me. I hate long queues at the checkout particularly when they have 50 tills and 10 tills open. When I am very old and there is a long queue to pay I am going to say to one of the assistants that I am incontinent and if I don't get served in the next 5 minutes I will piss on the floor. And I would! My view is that as you get older you can get away with more things. I see it as a curve that you can get away with lots of things when you are very young but that right goes down until you reach 70 then you can do what you like. I am definitely going to pretend to lose my passport on the plane when I arrive at UK immigration and see what happens.

On a quick note I must tell you a little story which emphasises the different way I think. I was on a motorbike tour of France and Germany. Being part of the European Union but not part of Schengen the only place you have to queue for passport control is leaving or entering the UK. I met another biker on the Shuttle from Calais to the UK. He told me that he had lost his passport in the Netherlands on the way back to Calais. He, like most British people, spent time going to the British Embassy and spending over £100 to just get a temporary passport and he would have to spend over another £100 to get a proper 10-year passport. I would have turned up at UK passport control at Calais and I would have given them my photo-card driving licence, if that had not been acceptable I would have said to the immigration official that he/she had 2 choices either accept it or turn to the page on the computer system that talks about what to do if someone claims asylum - I would have done that! It would have been interesting to see what would have happened. That is how I think differently. There are many examples of this in my life.

The American I met in a coffee shop was a bit weird. He was a paranoid schizophrenic. He had no chance. The main reason he was in Thailand was because marijuana was very cheap compared to the USA. I felt sorry for him and asked my Thai wife to help him and I invited him to stay with us. I felt sorry for him. We helped him find an apartment in the centre of Chiang Mai and arranged a local Thai woman to come in weekly to clean and do his laundry. We left for the UK and did not hear from him after a couple of months. I think a year later his family got in touch with me by email to tell me that he had died. I don't think he committed suicide but part of the problem is that I don't think he could live on his own. My 1st wife (who was English) once said to me that I was the only person she knew that would be happy on a desert island on my own.

In some ways that is true. I value my time on my own. I also like to ride my motorbike on my own as I hate to have someone on the back. You have to be responsible for them and stop when they need to and they might also want to talk to you. I go to China on my own to teach and I like being on my own. When I get home at night I don't have to speak to someone or take into account their feelings. I think this is a reaction to my 1st wife who was very needy and needing affirmation. She needed entertainment all the time - we were just incompatible on holiday as I could just lie there and do nothing on holiday while my 1st wife needed someone to talk to. I am a great people watcher and in Thailand there are a lot of different people to watch when you are sitting in a café in a busy part of Bangkok (the capital of Thailand).

There is a difference between the type of people that live and work in Thailand and the type of people who live and work in China. There are a number of different types - let me go into a couple.

The 1st type is the person running away from the UK - they have got divorced. They have lost almost everything. They are running away from their life in the UK. They have failed in the UK

The 2nd type is the lecher. He sees Thailand as a cornucopia of lovely woman and ladyboys. He is allowed to have sex with anything. He can have sex with women; ladyboys and very young girls however old and ugly he is. If you have my money in Thailand you can have anything you want and no one condemns or stops you. It is very difficult to get arrested as the Thai people don't want to lose access to easy money. It is a mutually beneficial arrangement. I make no moral judgement is that I think it is difficult to condemn what is going on in someone else's culture.

Type 3 has not made up their mind about what they want to do in life. They ill hang out at the bars - enjoy the cheap beer; cheap women and cheap drugs. There are rules in Thailand about things but the people of Thailand will ignore them. Every so often the Police will set up a roadblock to catch people not complying with the laws - the most popular roadblock is catching people not wearing a helmet. Easy for the police to make money. Or the police will crack down on something if the newspapers have brought it to people's attention after a bad accident or murder.

Foreigners (or Falangs) are seen by local women in Thailand as hitting the jackpot. They hit the jackpot either though making a lot of money as a sex escort or marrying a boyfriend. You have to remember that Thailand is very poor in comparison to the UK. Thailand has the same population as the UK but the economy is a sixth of the UK. In theory, UK people are 6 times than Thai people but Thai people are even poorer as they don't have free health care; proper pensions; disability help; unemployment benefit; workers' rights which we take for granted in Europe. Thai workers are treated like American workers!

When I first came to Thailand to visit the future wife Nicky I soon worked this out. As I have said I am good at understanding systems and was a hacker at some point. My quickest hack was the time it took me to type the password. I can't hack any more as you need to keep up to date with systems and how they change. I understood nearly every system and knew their back doors. I also the most common hacks - such as setting up dummy logins on networks so I can just dial in and log in. That one probably still works as there is usually a large turnover of IT staff in any company and companies have more logins than staff as they don't have enough staff to properly maintain the database of logins. As usual companies in the UK and the USA know this and know the dangers to your personal data but are not interested as it costs money and they can just make an excuse if your data is compromised.

Why did my wife 1st come to the UK and end up as a prostitute? It was a choice. It was recommended by her Aunt. Who had done the same work in Scotland. My wife divorced her 1st husband in Thailand and never received any money from him. She was expected to support her 2 daughters and her parents and herself. She had a good job in Chiang Mai in the North of Thailand but it was not enough. She was a manager of a store in a major chain called Tops. You would think she would have good prospects but the money wasn't enough and she decided to come to the UK. As I have shown earlier you can earn a lot being a prostitute in the UK.

Fortunately she could already speak English to quite a good standard before she came to the UK. She had been used as the translator to help the representatives from the Netherlands who were visiting on behalf of the Dutch holding company. She was assigned to help them as she was the best speaker of English. She not only helped them around the company but also accompanied them when they went out in the evening. She helped arrange bar girls to go back to their rooms.

She did this for the American as well. The American was staying with us and wanted to know where to find a girl so I and my wife offered to help. So we went on a little tour of Chiang Mai visiting a couple of bars that foreigners would not know about. She was negotiating on behalf of the American. A lot of inexperienced Thai bar girls don't want foreigners because they have been told stories of how big foreigners are (I am not talking about being fat!). Eventually found a local girl (Of course I assured them he was very small so they had nothing to worry about!). It was arranged she would visit the American the next night. The girl phoned my wife from the American's room and asked when she should ask for the money. My wife assured her that he would pay the next morning. The American in one bar said to me that it was like going with your mother to find sex.

My wife is very unusual for a Thai woman as she is not short. She is actually taller than a lot of men in Thailand. The reason for this is that her Grandfather was very tall as he was from China. I find it amazing that my wife, along with most Thai, hates Chinese people in general. She is part Chinese as are a lot of Thai people in the North of Thailand. A lot of Chinese people visit the North of Thailand and particularly Chiang Mai as it is possible to drive from China to Thailand in the North as they are quite close.

So we have the house and I stayed for 4 months in Thailand sorting out the house. There were the usual things to do. However the most important thing I did but I didn't know it was important until now was to contact a lawyer in Thailand to arrange a contract to be drawn between my wife and myself. As usual I did some research on the Internet about ownership of property in Thailand and discovered that foreigners could not own Land. However I found out that you could protect your investment as a foreigner in a couple of ways - one was though a lease contract or to set up a company to own the property. This is across the whole of Asia - I do not understand why we allow foreigners to buy property in the UK without any issue or restriction yet British people can't buy property without restriction in Asia. It is the same with passports - we allow Thai people to obtain a British passport but it is impossible for a British person to get a Thai passport!

I contacted a lawyer in Chiang Mai to protect my investment. Thank God or Buddha or whatever God that I did as it meant years later in my divorce that I keep the house. The lawyer divided the 5m baht price (about £86,000 then 5m baht now is about £135,000 - just shows how much poorer British people are because of Brexit!) into a 4m baht loan to my wife and 1m baht lease payment from me to my wife. It stated in the contract that I had paid the lease payment. I know how the lawyer came to that split but I won't say in this book as my wife has forgotten the reason for it and it would have helped her. But I am not going to tell her the reason for the split. It was a very good job I did this as I am sure I would not have had a home in Thailand and my money would have gone. The lease was for 30 years with a promise to put in place a lease for another 30 years. I was about 45 at the time so this meant that the lease would be in place until at least I was 75 - I might be dead before then.

Particularly as I ride a motorbike and I take more risks as I have got older. For me ride or die is a true belief. I would hate never to be able to ride a motorbike. I have always said to people that I would hate to die in my sleep if I am going to die I want to be on my motorbike at the time. I don't whether you have seen Sons of Anarchy and American series that followed a fictional motorbike gang in a fictional town in America. It was a Shakespearian tragedy as it was impossible to avoid the fate of his father whatever he tried to do. In the final scene he rides Jesus like into the path of a heavy truck on the motorway to atone for his sins and to protect his sons from the same fate. That is the way to go - on your motorbike on a sunny day.

I never want to die in my sleep. I once read that most older people die in their sleep between the hours of 3 and 4am in the morning. It appears that is when your blood pressure is at its lowest; your heart is at its lowest heart rate and your breathing is at its lowest. If that is the case then I think I will set an alarm every morning when I reach that age for 3am in the morning and go back to sleep at 4am. I think of anything worse than going to sleep and never waking up again.

You also have lots of very fit people who are dead who couldn't escape their genetic destiny. A man died at the age of 40 who was a marathon runner. His father died at 40 and his grandfather died at 40. So all that exercise and no enjoyment in the good things in life was for nought. I am relying on genetics. My family comes from peasant stock so is a perfect example of Darwin's theory at=t work. Any bad gene was not allowed to be passed on as my ancestors had no access to health care and good food. They were peasants - at the bottom of the food chain in England. My parents are still alive at 84 - as I say to my brother this bodes well for us. My parents have had a bad diet; have never exercised and very hard physical labouring jobs in factories. I would hope that with the good health care I have access to and received; the goodish diet and working in an office and not working too many long hours will mean that I will live even longer.

I am determined to be the oldest English man in existence one day. The main reasons for this are that firstly I want to get my monies worth from the pensions I have. After the 2008 financial crash in the UK the Government decided to support Bankers - they kept their pensions and their bonuses and had a tax cut as well. The rest of us had our pensions reduced; our pay cut and our tax go up. Not a whimper of protest by the British people - never underestimate the stupidity of the British. So I intend to get that money back by living as long as possible. Secondly, when the BBC interview me as they always do when someone is the oldest Briton alive I am sure they will ask me how long I have managed to stay alive so long and I will say because I fucking left the UK 70 years ago and also because of great sex! A man in a retirement home In America was kicked out of the home because one morning the staff found 2 sex escorts in his room - what is wrong with that? He deserved a fucking medal at 85!

As a British person when you travel you discover how bad the UK is. The right-wing media and the people in the UK (who don't travel) speak about the UK like it is the modern-day Camelot when the reality is far from that. All aspects of life in the UK are hard and unpleasant. Travelling to work - expensive; in crowded trains and with frequent late arrivals. At work - the worst rights of any country in Western Europe and the longest hours. Health care - the UK spends less on healthcare than any other nation in Western Europe. Pensions - the latest state retirement age and the worst pensions. Terrible customer service - I can guarantee not all cash desks will ever be open in a store - I just walk out at times.

In some ways, I am looking forward to being old as a man you can get with a lot more things than when you are a young man. For instance, you can be unpleasant in stores. My plan in UK stores if there is a big queue and only one cash desk is to accost a staff member and tell them that if I don't get served soon I will have to piss on the floor as I am incontinent. I also want to try pretending that I have lost my passport when I arrive in the UK and see what happens. Say to the UK Immigration official - Son I haven't seen you for a long time where have you been? I also can't wait to be the 1st on planes as they have all these notices stating that if you are old you can get on first on the plane. The problem is I haven't worked out how old you need to be to do that - is 60; 70 or 80? Also as an old man you can get away with more things with women.

Chapter 8 The marriage

We got married in Chiang Mai in Thailand.

After 4 months I returned to the UK to set up a new rented flat that my wife's friend had arranged. My wife and her friend had first met when my wife started as a prostitute as they were working together. The flat was in Wembley and was a 2 bedroom flat on the ground floor. It was not what I had asked Rose to arrange as it was in the middle of a busy junction but it was not very far from the tube so it had some advantages. When I arrived at London Heathrow it was quite late. From Bangkok to London it takes about 12 hours. I hate the flight as I cannot sleep. I have tried to take tablets; drink, and even try Business Class. None works so I have given up flying Business Class as I don't gain from it. Sleeping tablets did work on one flight but trying to get them from my GP in the UK was very difficult. I went to ask for a repeat prescription 9 months after the 1st 7 tablets I was given - I don't think you can get addicted to them on just 7 - perhaps I am wrong. The GP interrogated me - was I scared of flying - No; why did I go to Thailand and not Europe; was I addicted - No etc. Then he wanted me to tell him the name of the actual sleeping tablets from 9 months earlier - who the fuck knows that! I was only trying them because they seemed to work on the flight to Bangkok for 12 hours in an uncomfortable seat in a noisy smelly plane. I don't think it is too much to ask! So I gave up.

I arrived with just my luggage from Thailand so needed the usual stuff - tea; milk; food etc. So I asked the taxi driver to stop and you would think I was asking for the moon. The flat was OK and it had the Tube and shops nearby,

I sorted out the flat and Nicky then joined me a couple of days later, The reason she was a couple of days later is because there was only 1 seat on the plane left and the charge for it in Economy was 3 times the normal fare so it was cheaper to come 2 days later in Business Class. I was due back at work in the Met Police a week later. I and Nicky (my wife) started to sort out the flat - sort out Wi-Fi and cable TV etc.

In the meantime, I started to send money to pay the household expenses in Thailand and to support her daughters. Unfortunately, the real father has never provided a penny of support then and since then, I started to send £700 per month as the eldest stepdaughter was at University and there were fees to pay. A quite high level of support considering they had not and were not receiving anything from their real father. Part of that money sent was to pay that part of the mortgage that wasn't covered by the rent. The shortfall was only about £50 per month. However, I soon found out that I was expected to pay water charges I was not aware of that when I agreed to the rental for the 2 houses. I have to admit I took my eye off the ball in Thailand as I trusted my wife and I was very busy in the UK with work and looking for a flat in West London.

I was working in the Met Police as an accountant in the central finance function. When I first joined the Met Police in 2003 it was a good time to join. The Met Police was being properly funded by the Government and the Greater London Authority. The Met Police was also trying to change its culture from a mildly fascist organisation to a more open and inclusive organisation. It was also trying to get rid of the racist and sexist attitudes that had been in the Met Police since its inception. It was changing which was good.

It was a strange culture in the Met Police. I soon figured out that the Finance Dept. was run by a ruling clique. At first, I was welcomed into this clique and when there was a reorganisation I was offered whatever job I wanted and there were plenty of jobs as the Met Police had a problem in recruiting professionals. The pay being offered wasn't as good as the private sector and there were no benefits.

The Met Police had recognised that it needed to recruit proper accountants into the Finance Dept. after a debacle concerning the budget. One year the forecasts prepared had shown that the Met Police would be enormously overspent so they brought in emergency measures. Unfortunately, the forecast was totally wrong and nonsensical. The problem was they had Police officers and unqualified staff trying to do complex forecasts which was a recipe for disaster. I was part of a large group of accountants they brought into the Met Police. By the time I left after 12 years, I was one of the few left - every other accountant had left from that group.

When I joined the Met Police I was with my 1st wife (who was English) she saw the job at the Met Police as though all her Christmases had come. Her father had been in the Civil Service since the 2nd World War and she saw that as a proper job - security; pension and status. I also started at a level that was higher than her father ever achieved so my status went up in her eyes. Those jobs I had as an accountant were no good even though I had built a system in a startup; improved systems in other companies or ran a subsidiary in a national company in the UK.

I early discovered in my career that I was no good at detail and dealing with transaction processing. My skills were in systems; managing people and negotiating. I had helped set up new companies by joining when there were only 6 people at the company. I had written customer service systems and accounting systems using MS Access (the database module of MS Office); I had set up Networks; Accounting systems; HR systems and I had provided training in the use of systems. Because of my skills at understanding systems I quickly became a very good hacker. I could hack into all systems. The key to hacking then and probably still is is having knowledge of how IT software works. Also then a lot of software had back doors to get in - a password that was the default. As a result of my experience at hacking I find computer games very boring. There are only 2 games that I have enjoyed - Grand Theft Auto (GTA) and Doom.

When I worked in the NHS as Financial Controller at Ealing Hospital (while I was married to my 1st wife) a group of us used to play Doom over the hospital network. That was great fun! Other computer games available today don't do anything for me so I don't bother.

I am very good at using computers. I can combine and see the problems between 2 systems very quickly. I can picture the data in my head and remember what bits are missing. Before Windows you had to type in the commands to combine and check 2 databases and that is where I honed my skills at seeing information. I improved my skills at finding information - I suppose you would call data mining. This skill has been very useful in the divorce. I understand where data comes from and the weaknesses of the system.

Although the Met Police was trying to modernise its attitudes the problem it faced was that too many people had become institutionalised and gone native in their attitudes. The Met Police was a quasi militaristic organisation and that was reflected in the way people dealt with each other in the organisation. It also explains why it is slow to change and why cover-ups can happen. People in the organisation both Police Staff and Police Officers see their loyalty to the group they are in then the organisation and then to the people outside the organisation.

Police Staff are everyone else who are not Police Officers. Police Officers as a group are racist; sexist, and take the attitude that it is a Them and Us. Police Staff are supposed to provide expertise and control with regard to the behaviour of the organisation. Police Staff are made up of accountants; lawyers; IT staff; Human Resources etc.

The problem is that most of the Police Staff had gone native as they had been there for over 20 years. Because of the ruling clique who handed out promotions, it was not a good idea to rock the boat. Not a good idea to question or oppose what was going on. There are 3 examples of this that illustrate the point.

1. Police Staff would use "Sir" and "Ma'am" when dealing with someone that was a senior manager or Police Officer. Someone even said it to me when I phoned them up. I have never in an office environment called anyone Sir or Ma'am. I have worked in large multinational companies and never called anyone that even the Chief Executive. Throughout my career I have only heard people use first names when communicating in an office.

2. There was a big scandal in the Met Police concerning the use of credit cards by Police Officers. Some Police Officers were given American Express cards to use for expenses. This made sense if a Police Officer is undercover - it would make no sense for a Police Officer undercover having to submit an expense form for each week. There were rules that needed to be followed and they were straightforward. Each month the Police officers would be sent an

itemised bill and they indicated what expenses were personal. If they didn't do this then after 3 months it would be assumed that all the expenses were personal and the whole lot would be deducted from pay - very simple. The accountants based in each Met Police borough were supposed to police the system. But they didn't. So Police Officers took advantage of that and just used the American Express as I free resource for paying for personal items. The personal items included buying sex toys and arranging for Rose petals to be sprinkled over a hotel bed for someone's mistress. When it surfaced the attitude was taken that there was a problem with the rules which let off the Police Officers involved - a lot had the money written off and most did not have to pay back the money straight away. The rules were simple it was just a combination of the militaristic culture and going native by the accountants who were supposed to be policing the system. The militaristic culture meant they felt they could not question a "superior" officer.

3. Most people in the Met Police had been there for 20 years. They had come straight from school and so during their formative years were being moulded by the Met Police culture. People in the Met Police were not promoted because of their skills but it was based on fitting in. That results in no one questioning the culture. That is why the culture was perpetuated forever in the Met Police. A good example of this is a senior police officer who came to me as I was well known in the Met Police as a Trade Union rep to support a member of Police Staff (not civilians as they are sometimes called) who had been racially abused by a senior police officer. The Black woman was a PA for the perpetrator of the incident. The police officer one day decided to put a banana down his trousers and run around the office making

monkey noises at his Black PA. Now do not tell me that he had not been racist in the past and that people did not know this as they were promoting him. The Met Police was prepared to promote you even if you were racist; sexist and misogynist as long as your face fitted. People were promoted on the basis that they were one of the lads - going drinking every week; sharing the same views and being useful in carrying the briefcase of a senior manager to the manager's car for them!

I could never fit into that culture - I saw too much bullying when I was at school. I cannot stand bullies. Also coming from my background where you start out with every disadvantage including my parents never buying me a serious book apart from comic books such as the Beano; Wizard etc - I bought the serious books from the money I earned as a child. Also my parents believed that my only ambition should be to work on a production line in a factory. And moving around the Midlands in England many times before the age of 7. A lot of people because of this background would end up in drugs or crime but I think I was saved by my intelligence; my scepticism about most claims by people; my stubbornness and my school.

I went to school in the late 60s and 70s. This was a different time to now. Exams were not that important and there were plenty of jobs available at all levels of qualification. I remember in the 70s a big headline when unemployment reached 1m - now we accept much higher levels. The unemployment figure now is not comparable as there have been so many revisions that you can't compare the two figures.

School in the 70s was good for me. I did lots of sport and I learnt a lot from teachers who were given the freedom to teach - there were no targets and assessments. We had to share textbooks because of the IMF(International Monetary Fund) intervention but education was good for me. I was lucky that they had abolished the 11+ a couple of years before I started school as I would have ended up in a secondary modern school and fulfilled my destiny by ending up at a car factory on the production line. I read Shakespeare for the 1st time and I listened to Classical Music for the 1st time. This happened in a Rural Studies lesson. Yes, we had Rural Studies (which was compulsory) as we were based in a rural market town surrounded by farms. I learnt about crop rotation and the killing of animals. We were taken to farms and shown the process for turning a live animal into sausages. It never caused me nightmares. I find it very funny when people complain about the killing of animals for our burgers - where do people think their cheeseburger comes from?

I was difficult at school. I questioned everything and I was naughty with pranks and jokes. I think if I am bored I deliberately do something to liven things up - this carried on into my work life.

So we had returned to the UK and I was working at the Met Police as an accountant and Trade Union rep. Money was being sent to Thailand to pay household expenses and to help the stepdaughter with University costs. I bought a flat in West London and decided to bring the youngest stepdaughter over to the UK to live with us. This would give her more opportunities to study and work. She was about 20 when she came. I applied for a visa for her and at first it was refused. I arranged the appeal.

That was an interesting experience. We were given a time and date at the main Immigration courts in West London. I was surprised we were herded into a courtroom at the appointed time with about 10 other people. As soon as we sat down the Government lawyer came over and asked if I was Mr. Vale and then she stated that the British Embassy in Thailand had decided not to oppose the appeal and was granting the visa. I was a bit disappointed as I had prepared a very good closing for the judge and had also coached my wife to cry when she was talking about missing her daughter. A bit disappointing. But the visa was granted.

So life went along. I was sending money each month and visit Thailand when I could. You have to remember Thailand is 12 hours flight away so it is not a weekend trip. My wife was not working at first. She seemed to enjoy the life. I was paying for everything and she had access to a joint bank account that I paid all my income to without any contribution from my wife.

However, her demands began to escalate and then I found out that she had sold a House I invested in without telling me. I found it out in my usual way by asking questions and working out some of it by myself. I had invested in 2 more houses on a different development just down the road from the main house in Doi Saket, Chiang Mai in Thailand. The total cost was £20k for 2 houses next door to each other. I borrowed £10k from the Thai bank which meant I was risking only 10k. I was interested to see if it was worth investing in property in Thailand in terms of return and capital growth. The cost of the loan was 9,200 baht (approx. £170 at that time) per month. My wife found the renters at 9,000 baht per month for both houses. Looking back I think she lied about that as I am now renting out the main house for 25,000 baht now so I think now that she was keeping 50% of the rent and not telling me. The reason I think that now is what she said at the time when she asked me if 9,000 baht rent was enough! My view at the time and the reason why I didn't ask any more questions was that I knew nothing about the rental market in Doi Saket in Thailand and I trusted my wife - perhaps that was silly of me. It was only later that I found out that I was expected to pay the water charge which I found out later was a bit odd as I am now renting out my house in Thailand and the renters pay all the bills including the water charges. Looking back I think she lied to me. This was about 2 to 3 years after we had married.

I had accepted the deal that I would pay for things as she came from a poor family. She was also expected to give money to her parents and daughters. As I have said her brother (Ampol Tharaso) never gave any money to support his parents and expected support from his sister, my wife.

My wife and I were based in the UK. We were living in the flat I had bought in West London. After about 2 years my wife said she would like a dog. So we bought a chocolate Labrador puppy. It was quite big (I am not going to use the pronoun "he" for a dog because the pronouns "he" and "she" only refer to people - it annoys me when people don't remember that). She wanted some company during the day as I was out at work. I went to work by motorbike which my wife did not understand as she thought I was crazy going through London to work. I found using a motorbike the best way to go to work as it was the most cost-effective and quickest way of getting to work.

In the early years of our marriage my wife got breast enlargement. I think it was my wife's idea and, of course, I had no problem with that. She went from a 34B to a 34d - very nice and they looked very real. There were no stitches to see as the surgeon in Thailand went through the armpit - very clever. Anyway sometime after the operation we were with friends one evening - Thai female friends of my wife. At that get together my wife decided to let her friends feel her breasts to see that they felt real. I stayed very quiet hoping that they wouldn't notice I was there. Who doesn't love as a man women touching other women's breasts?

We brought over the youngest daughter (Vissanee Laowanit - Lek) to the UK and she was living with us. This happened about 2012. My wife wanted the youngest daughter to come to the UK because the youngest daughter was very lazy at school and wasn't achieving anything. My wife thought that her daughter would have more opportunities. I as I talked about earlier arranged this and paid for it.

I find it surprising, and I haven't heard of this before, that my wife's daughters are bisexual and lesbian. The eldest daughter Ploy is bisexual and the youngest daughter, Lek, is lesbian. The reaction of people in the UK when they found this out was surprising at times. Sometimes people would say that it must be difficult and some found it a turn on. I didn't think much about it. I am very liberal in views, despite my working-class background, and took the view that people can like whatever they like in sex as long as people consent to what is going on.

It was interesting that, in my opinion. They picked ugly girlfriends. The girlfriends were very spotty and looked more like teenage boys than girls. I did say to the stepdaughters (me being me) - couldn't they have picked prettier girlfriends? I never received an answer! The girlfriends were quite nice but they were a bit boring. Lek's girlfriend moved in with us and lived in the step daughter's room. I treated the girlfriend as part of the family.

The girlfriend came on holiday with us and stayed with me at home when the stepdaughter was working. Lek was working in a Thai restaurant in Ealing. She worked in the afternoon and evenings until quite late. I didn't ask the girlfriend or Lek to contribute to the expenses of the flat so they lived with us for free - rent-free and expenses free. I even paid for food for us all. I also continued to pay the expenses of the house in Thailand and support the eldest daughter.

In 2010 the coalition government came into being. The Conservative party and the Liberal Democrats decided to form a coalition - as usual, the Liberals did not learn from the lessons of history. The Coalition government then introduced austerity measures and announced that there would be staff cuts across the whole of the Public Sector, which of course I was working in as I worked for the Met Police. The coalition in the following years introduced pay freezes for 3 years in the Public Sector and increased to cost of pensions in the Public Sector whilst people in the Banking sector who had taken £400bn of public money didn't see any increase in tax or pension costs.

At that point I decided that I was not going to stay in the Public Sector. My view was that I have earned my skills and experience and an organisation needs to pay for them - I don't take a pay cut. So I began my campaign to be made redundant and take my pension early - as you could take it from 50 if made redundant.

From 2010 to 2015 I went out of my way to be a pain through my Union work and do as little work as possible in my job as an accountant to get redundancy. Also the work became very boring. It was like being on a production line - if I wanted to be on a production line I would have been working in a factory as my parents wanted when I was 16. When I joined the Met Police we were trying to improve systems in order to support policing but with the introduction of austerity and the appointment of Hogan-Howe, as Commissioner, there was no interest in improving systems but just the saving of money. I always find it funny the British complain about their public services but are not prepared to pay for them. The British also have this view that people in the public sector should not get paid or have a pension - as there are continual complaints about the public sector pension arrangements by the media and the public.

As a result of the cuts in budgets to the Met Police the organisation started to go through multiple reorganisations in the Finance Dept. Instead of every year, it became a regular routine of reorganisation every 3 months. It wasn't helped by the attitude of Hogan-Howe, the new Commissioner, that he had stated that the Met Police had no problem meeting the target of achieving its targets with 25% less money;25% less staff and 25% less crime. I find it ironic in 2019 that he is suddenly stating that the cuts in funding for the police service resulted in a rise in crime.

My wife and I were getting along and everything seemed fine. We went on trips to Europe like skiing. It was quite funny skiing. We went to Chamonix in France - I normally go Val d'Isere but I wanted to try Chamonix as the rich and famous seem to go there. I like Val d'Isere as it is quite a small town in a perfect location as you can ski right into the town. In Chamonix I booked ski lessons for the wife and I would go off on the runs down the mountain. I went to meet my wife after her lesson and I couldn't find her. Eventually I went back to the hotel and she was buried under about 3 duvets; coats and had her winter clothes on in bed. She was very cold - me I thought it was lovely. Clearly shows the difference between Thai and North European people.

We also travelled to Paris and Venice and Rome. I also went on motorbike holidays in Western Europe. I have been all over Western Europe on my motorbike. I prefer motorbikes to cars. Cars to me are just boxes on wheels - a Ferrari and a Mini look the same to me.

The stepdaughter and her girlfriend who were living with us permanently were very lazy. They did nothing in the flat.

They didn't do any cleaning; washing; ironing; shopping for food and zero contribution to costs. My wife and I went on holiday once and left the stepdaughter in charge. When we came back the flat was spotless - I was amazed and told her she had done a good job. A couple of days later we found out the truth that while we had been away the stepdaughter had done nothing even leaving back garden very dirty as the dog used it as a toilet and the stepdaughter had not cleared up any of the mess from the dog. It appeared the friend, Rose Matthews, had come in and cleaned the flat for us and cleaned up the back garden. The stepdaughter had not told us this but accepted the thanks. I think that sums up the attitude of the stepdaughters.

We went back to Thailand as often as possible. I have a house in Thailand and the weather is good the whole year around. The temperature in Chiang Mai never goes below 25C and you know what the weather is going to be - there are only 2 seasons per year rainy and dry. It can be quite funny watching the weather forecasts in Thailand as for 6 months of the year the weather forecast for the next day is rain and for the next 6 months the weather forecast is for dry and sunny. That is one of the attractions of Thailand for me as I am fed up with the weather in the UK - always changeable and you can never predict the weather in the UK. It pisses me off along with the stupidity of the British.

Why do I think the British are stupid? There are many reasons but some of them are the following:

1. Always talking about the war - every month I can predict that a politician or person on the street will mention the war. Even worse with Brexit going tits up.

2. Always wanting he British Empire back - for God's sake grow up! The rest of Europe has accepted that they can't have an empire back and concentrated on improving the lives of their citizens. This is one of

the reasons we keep wasting money to support the USA in their stupid wars in the Middle East.

3. The British are experts at self-delusion - the British believe that they have the best health service in the world; the most generous benefits system in the world and the best pensions in the world. The British don't like facts getting in the way of a good story. In fact the French health service is better; pensions are better in the rest of Western Europe and finally the UK has the worst benefits system in Western Europe

4. Customer service - customer service must be the worst in the world and the British accept it. Companies will give silly reasons and lie to you and the British accept it. Companies know this and set up their systems to just put someone by lying to them knowing that 80% will go away and not pursue it.

Some newspaper columnist said that Britain is just one big train station full of people hoping to go somewhere better.

This is shown by a survey that is done every year by the European Union. The basic question is where would you live if you were given a large amount of money. The British consistently state, more than any other country, that they would live somewhere else in the world. It is estimated that 10m British people live permanently outside the UK. Sums up the problems in the UK really! I am one of the lucky ones - I have escaped.

So we are having a good time - as far as I know. Then in 2010 my wife states she wants to work. She gets a job with a Thai massage place. My wife has done some training and is very good as she practised when she was a prostitute. Obviously, it wasn't all massage when she was a prostitute. The company she chose to work for Nuad Thai (which means Thai massage in Thai). They had a number of stores in North West London. I was later to find out that they ran an immigration scam. There were 2 elements to the scam:

1. The promised women in Thailand a job working at one of their shops. They also promised accommodation but for this opportunity the women had to pay up to £20,000 to get the job. When they arrived the accommodation was one of the massage rooms at the shop - there was no heating. I am sure that the company did a deal with officials at the British Embassy to get visas for them. This what happens at the British Embassy in Bangkok. The visa service has now been outsourced and it is probably even worse. I find it funny when people in the UK talk about immigration from the EU but don't worry about immigration from South East Asia where you can buy a visa. I was told the story of the German man who was deported from Thailand who was then given a visa by the very same immigration official who had deported him!

2. Wages: the company paid the staff in cash and no tax or NI was paid. This practice is rife in the Thai massage business. I know this because I talk to other Thai people. Thai massage businesses in the UK cannot afford to pay staff minimum wage or the living wage. The model does not and cannot work. I am very surprised that HMRC (UK Tax Government dept) has not investigated this industry - it could recover millions in lost tax evasion. It is a terrible industry as it takes advantage of vulnerable poor women who do not know any of the rules or rights that they have. And the woman pays to come and work there. Nuad Thai was making a fortune from this scam. Nearly all the Thai massage shops do the same practices.

In 2014, to everyone's surprise, I was elected President of the main Police Staff union in the Met Police. Even though I was looked upon with horror by the Met Police as I was the 1st left-wing President of the Union. My view was that the Union had to take a more confrontational style as the Met Police had changed along with the Public Sector, The coalition Government of Conservatives and Lib Dems had ushered in an era of cuts and those cuts in the Met Police involved managing disabled staff out of the organisation. I found that disgusting and was even more disgusted that managers used the Nuremberg excuse to try and justify their actions. I was under the threat of redundancy which was not a threat as I wanted it. I was not prepared as I have already said for the organisation to have the advantage of my skills at a discount. I always said to Union members you should not be grateful for a job but the Met Police should show its gratitude for you working for the organisation. The view is that the Met Police ensured that I left the Met Police - I was glad of that as I was not prepared to see my living standards being reduced for the benefit of Bankers!

In 2014 I was made redundant. Even though they reduced my pension as I was taking it early it still meant that I could live in it in Thailand if I needed to. I was also expecting to live to a very old age as both my parents are still alive at the age of 84. I have always said to my brother that that is good as it bodes well for us. I had already planned to take the TEFL exam to become an English teacher in Asia.

I had been involved in training throughout my career. I had started in Teaching as I went to teacher training college after I left school but then moved into Accounting. I had provided training in IT; HR; accounting systems and the use of spreadsheets. I had always enjoyed teaching and it was a natural fit for my skills. The plan agreed with my wife was that I would teach in Asia for about 5 years and then we would retire totally. I could save money in China teaching as I would be getting a free apartment.

I knew that my wife was lying to me about the monthly expenses for the house in Thailand. I paid for a housekeeper which cost about 6,000 baht per month about £100 then). It was a good deal as she came 5 days a week and did everything in the house - she even cleaned the car for me. When I was there on my own she would cook me breakfast - an English breakfast, of course - and would get me fruit and lunch as well. She was very good. And very cheap. I don't think you could get a full-time housekeeper for just over £100 in the UK. I accepted that my wife was skimming some money but I took the view that expenses would vary and also when I went to Thailand every year food would be ready for me when I arrived. I should be able to trust my wife, shouldn't I?

On my 1st divorce from my wife in the UK I received a settlement of £350,000 which meant that I was able to restart my life. I had already decided to marry my Thai girlfriend as she seemed a perfect fit for me. She was pretty; sexy; intelligent; a good cook and she had a traditional view of marriage. A woman who has a traditional view is quite important to me. I am not a man who is into discussing feelings for hours or knowing about "women's" things. A lot of women don't like that attitude and I have no problem with that. However there are still a lot of women in the world who want a man who is a man. What do I mean by that? I am a man who has high self-esteem - I don't value people's opinion of me unless I agree with it - I know my failings; I know what   I am good at and what I am bad at. I am not interested in knowing about women's periods as I will never use that information or the information be of use to me as I have 2 sons. I will make decisions but I will not be interested in feelings about that decision. Unfortunately women seem to think that I need to know such things and go into a great deal about these things. For example, in the Met Police I was representing a woman who was receiving IVF treatment she went into every detail about the procedure and the needles and the after-effects. My 2 wives have both wanted to share their periods with me - all the gory details and what it looks lie each month. I don't need to know! I also think there should be a man filter on adverts on TV.

I was able to restart my life after the 1st divorce. I bought a flat in London; I bought a house in Thailand for retirement; I bought a car in Thailand and UK and was able to buy furniture for the house in Thailand and the flat in the UK. It had taken 3 years the 1st divorce but it was worth it. What the other side in the divorce didn't know was that I was down to my last penny when we went to family court and finally came to an agreement. I could not have gone on as my credit had been reduced by the bank and credit card companies. The key though is to never let the other side know of your problems. One of the important strengths of my case in the 1st divorce was that my wife had been involved in tax evasion which I think is going to be important in the present divorce as it involves not only my wife but other people as well.

I paid 5m baht for my home in Thailand - £86,000 then. The house was 4 bedrooms and 3 bathrooms with a garden. I also bought a Toyota Hilux 4 wheel drive car or uit as they call it in Australia. That was very cheap compared to the UK as the same car would have probably been about £30,000 but I paid £17,000 in Thailand. A couple of years later I bought 2 houses on anew development just down the road for about £10k cash and a mortgage - this was to see if it was worth investing any further in the Thai property market.

I left the administration of our life in Thailand to my wife as I did not know much about the cost of things in Thailand and I did not understand the language at all. I was also busy in the UK with my career and sorting out the new flat and bills in the UK.

My wife decided that she wanted to work and go back to doing Thai massage. She started work with a company Nuad Thai that had 3 shops in West London. My wife went to work in 2 of them - in Ealing and Northwood. I quickly began to understand that they exploited the Thai woman working for them. They brought women over from Thailand who had paid for the privilege and then had them stay in the shop. I found out that the owners used the same accounting firm that specialised in looking for obscure tax loopholes and had made a name for themselves. Clearly, the Thai massage paid well, it pays more when you paying staff in cash and don't declare anything for tax so that they did not have to pay the minimum wage and pay employer taxes. The Thai woman did not realise they had rights.

Talking about money, The real father of my wife's daughters had never paid a penny to support his daughters yet had another family with children which he supported. My wife had never taken him to court to get maintenance which surprised me but I was to find out later the reason when I started to divorce my wife. My wife, so she said, had allowed him 3 affairs before she divorced him and she used to say to me that I was allowed 3 affairs. I took that with a pinch of salt. The daughters never saw their father and did not seem to want to,

The stepdaughters always came to me to ask me things they never discussed things with their mother. They, at first, wanted to know about the gay scene in the UK. They asked about lesbian bars and other things. I tried to give them support as I felt sorry for them as they had spent most of their lives living with grandparents rather than their parents. The reason for them living at their grandparents was because their mother worked in the city which was about 90 minutes away each way and the problem with work in Thailand is that you can be expected to work any hours.

My wife worked for a large supermarket group. She was the manager of a store in Chiang Mai so must have been paid relatively well in Thailand. However she still didn't have enough money as she was expected to support her parents and her children. Her aunt suggested she go to the UK to become a prostitute as the Aunt had been one and earned a lot of money.

My wife wanted to work 6 days a week in the massage shops. I had no issue with this as long as things were still done at home. She didn't have to work as we had a comfortable lifestyle and also she had sold some assets in Thailand without telling me.

I should have taken it as a warning side and treated it more seriously when I found out she had sold a motorbike I had bought in Thailand and one of the houses I had invested in without telling me. I decided not to do anything as the house sold I assumed had been used to pay off the loan. The motorbike was another thing. So later I cancelled my wife's access to my bank account. I only restored that just before we left for China. My wife's attitude that all the assets belong to her in Thailand has come more to the fore as we have gone through the divorce.

Chapter 9 Thailand

Why Thailand?

This a question I am asked a lot. I have alluded to why previously - the weather. I am surprised that most people when they retire in the UK stay there. It seems incomprehensible considering the low pensions in the UK and the weather. I have to admit that a big factor in my decision is that I met a Thai woman.

Thai culture is very different from Western culture. This the same all over South East Asia. The main reasons are as follows:

1. No tax on certain things - no council tax; no TV Licence; no water rates.

2. Less tax - VAT at a lower rate; car tax less; car insurance less; petrol tax less

3. Lower costs - petrol is 50% less than the UK; food costs lower; restaurants are cheaper; beer is cheaper.

4. More expensive - only a few things are more expensive like Western food in shops and restaurants e.g. beef. Cars from Europe are about double that of the West due to import tax.

5. Property prices - property to buy and rent is much lower than in the UK. You can still buy a house in Bangkok, the capital, for £55,000. This is a 3 bedroom house with 2 bathrooms on a new development. To rent - you can rent a 3 bedroom house in Bangkok near the main airport for £650 per month (because of the stupid decision of the British on Brexit 10 years ago the cost would have been £450 - inflation will go up in the UK soon!).

6. Climate - it is unlikely that you will freeze to death in Thailand. The weather never goes below 25 degrees. The locals think it is cold if it gets to 20 degrees. You do not need your winter clothes and the decision you have to take is which shorts shall I wear today?

7. Health care and dentists - I have found the doctors and dentists to be very good and very cheap. A check-up costs £20 including a clean and a filling costs £20 - much less than the so-called NHS dentistry in the UK (I call it that as we pay when we go to the dentist but don't pay when we go to a hospital – can someone explain please). My view is that if you have a big problem return to the UK but you need to make sure that the UK Government believes that you still live in the UK. There are ways to do that!

8. Thai women - what can you say. Very pretty and sexy and still believe that a woman's role is to look after her man. If you are a man you have many women to choose from- you can be enormously fat, hardly able to walk and ugly and you have your choice of women. You can choose from any age from 16 upwards. I am not interested in very young because they have no

shared experiences with me - they don't remember a time before the mobile phone. I am only interested in 40+ as they do have some shared experiences. The older woman is also better at looking after you as a man. It helps a man as there is still a stigma for an Asian woman if she is on her own after a certain age. In China, for instance, parents will go to a singles market on behalf of their children, who are over 26, to try and find a suitable partner for them. However I have seen very old men with very young women - women who are about 40 years younger. I have a theory that all women have Daddy issues. Most women are looking for a man that reminds them of their Daddy. I have to say I am very thankful that women are not like men as most men, me included, would never find a woman. I admit that I have been lucky in my life as I have never been out with an ugly woman - most of the time other men are wondering why the woman chose me.

9. Technology - the internet and cable TV are well provided for in Thailand. Everywhere you go you will find the Internet.

10. Corruption - this is the biggest difference between the West and Thailand. Police corruption is rife and, in my experience, is worse outside Bangkok as the Police in the provinces have more time to stop foreigners to get money out of them. I am always stopped in Chiang Mai on my motorbike but it has never happened in Bangkok. I like corruption - I find it works and it can make life easier. For instance, I once arrived in Thailand and my car had no tax; no insurance and no MOT. The police stopped me and it cost me £10 and they let me keep the car - in the UK the car would have been towed away and I would have faced a possible criminal case. I liked the Thai system.

11. Roads - I have to mention roads as I am a biker (motorbike). Bangkok is like any other capital city in the world - crowded; pollution; traffic jams. But when you get outside the capital you find the roads to be great. There are no motorways but the main roads between the cities are well maintained and easy to ride. All main roads have many service stations and cafés with internet access. Even the smallest roadside café has internet access so no problem. And of course it is very sunny in the dry season. It can be very wet on a motorbike in the rainy season. I found this out on one ride from Bangkok to Chiang Mai. The rain started in Bangkok and lasted for 300 km - unfortunately I had no waterproof trousers on. I was very wet very quickly - however as soon as it stopped raining and the sun came out the combination of sun and the wind soon dried off my trousers.

Overall I cannot see many problems with living in Thailand - if you are a man. I am not too sure what is available for a woman from the West as Thai society is still very patriarchal and I don't see how a marriage between a Western woman and a Thai man would work.

Chapter 10 Divorce

You now have a flavour of the background to the events leading up to the divorce. You understand Thailand a bit; you have formed a view of the main protagonists and you are probably thinking what caused the divorce as they seemed to be getting on fine. To me, it seemed as though we were getting on fine but then some things happened which meant that after 12 years we could not continue. Some of the people mentioned at the beginning have not been mentioned yet - that is because they come into play during the divorce.

As I have said earlier we moved to China at the end of February 2016 as I had been made redundant the year before in my job as an accountant in the Met Police. As I said I engineered that redundancy and retirement as the Government had decided that people in the Public Sector should subsidise the Bankers who had caused the financial crash that costs the UK taxpayer £400 billion (yes billion not million).

I had a job arranged in Ma'anshan near to Nanjing in China. The pay offered was near the bottom of the scale for teaching English in China but it was my 1st job and it came with a rent-free apartment. The plan was (which was agreed with my wife) was to try it for 5 years and then retire totally to Thailand and the house in Chiang Mai - the house I had bought.

There was a lot of sorting out in the 12 months leading up to the move to China. I had to sell my flat in London; arrange the disposal of items we couldn't take to China; arrange visas; pack everything and book flights. The biggest mistake I made was arranging the flight with British Airways Business Class. The seats were very uncomfortable and the seats were not in the best arrangement. I had a choice of Finnair but the travel agent said that British Airways was better - I wish I had not listened to him. The great thing about Business Class if you going a long distance is you get 96kg each of baggage in the hold. So we had 192kg of baggage with us for China.

I hate long flights as I can't sleep. I slept once after I took some sleeping tablets but the GP gave me such a hard time when I asked for some more for my next trip that I gave up. He asked me why I needed them; was I scared of flying; why did I go to Thailand; why didn't I go somewhere else - I just gave up I was only asking for 7 tablets. I have tried everything - I have tried Business Class; I have tried drinking and I have tried different times. None of this works and I am usually working up and down the plane or watching the same movie for the 3rd time to pass the time. I wish flying long-distance was like in the "Fifth Element" where they knock you out with gas and then wake you up when you arrive at your destination. The only problem with this is would you prefer to be woken up if the plane is going to crash or left asleep - I would prefer to be woken up! There are going to be similar problems with driverless cars - if the car has to make a choice between you and someone else in a life or death situation who do you want the car to save? Definitely me. Or do you want the car to decide on probability who to save? I look forward to the day the airline gives me drugs to sleep on a long flight.

So we had a long flight to China and were met at the airport however they had no car. This meant that we had to arrange for some of the suitcases to be delivered another day. We then had to trek across the city by tube. I was pulling 2 suitcases. That was interesting - no one would let you off the subway before getting on. You just had to put your head down and charge slowly. Being big helps in that situation. We then transferred to a car and taken to the new apartment in the city of Ma'anshan.

Unfortunately, the new apartment was on the 5th floor with no lift and was quite old. My wife thought it was very dirty but to me it just reminded of when I went to University and living in student digs. Student flats in the early 80s are not like today - today they have plush accommodation with en-suite etc. I think I am like most men we seem to have a problem noticing dirt. Most things were there that we needed but the bed did not have a mattress. I am not good at sleeping on a piece of wood. My wife was OK as she was Thai and used to sleeping on the floor when she was a child and a teenager. Being from the West I did not enjoy it. But I persevered until I bought a mattress on the Chinese version of Ebay.

It is interesting that China appears in documentaries as the modern economic superpower which is technologically advanced. It is in some ways but in others not. Take the toilets and sinks. The rest of the World uses a U bend and knows what width of pipe to use for the toilet. China in its own wisdom decided that it knew better than the rest of the world. So China takes a washing machine hose and connects the sink waste to a hole in the wall which I assume connects to the drain. I had a problem with the toilet early on my trip to China. As normal I put the toilet paper down the toilet and flushed. Then after 2 weeks it blocks and then people tell me you don't put toilet paper down the toilet as it will block the toilet. I worked out that the reason for this is that the toilet waste pipe is narrower than in the West and the rest of the World - why? Everyone knows that toilets block in China if you put toilet paper don the toilet so why not change it???

We also quickly discovered that you need a VPN for China as China has the great Firewall. It stops access to things like Casebook and Facebook and Youtube. It has invented its own equivalents but they don't work very well as the searches are censored so if you search for bbc.co.uk the search engine gives you all sorts of weird results. If you search for Fox News that is OK. This makes no sense as Fox News is a right-wing Trump-supporting news channel that hates China while the BBC has to present both sides of a discussion. Weird!

For my wife the major issue was not the toilets or the dirt or the Internet, the main issue for her was that everyone she met in China thought she was Chinese. Market stallholders and shop assistants would speak in Chinese to her expecting a reply but did not get one and looked at my wife as though she was mentally deficient.

I thought we were doing OK and apart from the small problems that she was OK but clearly was not. There were things going that I did not know about until the divorce really started going. Unfortunately for my wife, the further this process of divorce goes on the more information I can find about her behaviour and finances in Thailand. My greatest skill as an accountant was to find information and check against other sources. Most accountants when they begin their training work as auditors checking the accounts of companies and some accountants develop enormous skills in checking information and finding it. My skills are highly developed.

Chapter 11 My wife decided to take action

I have to admit that part of the reason for our divorce is my affair. I was having an affair but my plan was to end it when I began to find out things about the actions taken by my wife and her family. It is ironic that I was planning to end as life was too complicated. I don't like complicated and I wanted to make my life easier but then my life became more complicated. I think part of the reason for the attacks by my wife and her family was because I gave the appearance of being a pushover. But I am not as I have demonstrated at work and in my personal life - I appear very laid back perhaps I was too nice to my wife and her family so they thought that they could take what they wanted and I would just let them! I thought my wife had been a long time in the West, which she had, and would have learnt something from her 10 years in the UK. They forgot that some Western men are not like Thai people or perhaps they thought that I would just give up. I think some women have been emboldened by the weakness of a lot of men my age who give up in divorce. That annoys me and I do say it to men who have done that - one of them was John Hatfield the owner of Sansara Massage Limited where my wife was working. But we will come back to his role in the divorce.

Who are the main characters:

1.Main characters:

- Nicky (Somphorn) Vale (Tharaso) - wife

- Ploy Laowanit - stepdaughter

- Mitesh (Mac) Varsani

- John Hatfield

- Jane Doe - Nicky Vale best friend for 14 years

2.Minor characters:

- Pete Griffiths - teacher in China

- Vissanee Laowanit - youngest stepdaughter

A brief description of the main characters:

I have already spoken about Nicky (my wife) and Ploy. I will just give a flavour of Ploy. She has a degree and works for Bangkok Bank not only as a bank teller but as an investment advisor. She is very lazy and has no concept of money as she has always been given money by her mother. It is a familiar story nowadays where there are lots of spoilt children who have grown into entitled adults. Nicky did this as she felt guilty leaving them for so long when she had to go to the UK to be a prostitute in 2004 when the daughters were quite young. Mrs. Vale had a good job in Thailand as the manager of a branch of Tops supermarkets, a large group in Thailand. However because the real father did not provide any financial support she had to get more money and the only answer (suggested by her Aunt) was to go to the UK and work as a prostitute. Nicky also had to provide for her parents.

Nicky never sued her ex-husband for maintenance for the children and I always wondered about that as she needed the money. I eventually worked it out that the reason she did not sue the ex-husband for maintenance was because the ex-husband had given her brother - Ampol Tharaso - a job as a security guard after he came out of prison. The brother, Ampol, had been to prison for raping an 8 year old girl but had been released as a result of the King's birthday. Every year the King on his birthday would release prisoners. Clearly it would not be able to get a job as he had failed at school and was a child rapist.

John Hatfield - John involved himself in this when he decided to give a false statement to the court in the UK. He was Nicky's boss where she worked (or claimed to work) at Sansara Massage, which is based in Ruislip in West London. He had a history of being a weak man when it came to South East Asian women. He had been married twice to women from South East Asia and in both cases, when he divorced, he gave them all the assets and kept the debts. He is not the only one of a similar age to me who have done that - very annoying. He also lent some money to a Thai woman who was working at the company and she never paid him back - he did nothing even though he knew where she lived. He was also well known for employing Thai women and then try to get into bed with them by harassing them. My wife thought very little of him - she thought he was stupid and pathetic as he used to get upset with his Thai business partner in the business having a boyfriend - I have a message from my wife.

The involvement of John Hatfield in the Thai massage business was strange. The company was set up by the business partner who owned 100% of the company. John Hatfield was then appointed Director and only in February 2018 were all the shares transferred to him. The company was set up in June 2013 so John Hatfield who claims to have set up the company does not own any shares until February 2018 - nearly 5 years after the company set up - interesting? It suggests that there is a story on its own there.

John Hatfield's role seemed to be to do everything else associated with business apart from managing the business during the weekdays.

It all started because I found out that the stepdaughter Ploy Laowanit had been lying to me about repaying a loan and that my wife had colluded in that deception. My wife even sent me a message stating that her daughter had made payments each month and told me over the phone that it was happening. It was only 2,000 baht per month and no interest for a 300,000 baht loan. The loan was to help the stepdaughter buy her 1st apartment. 2,000 baht is about £40 per month. I feel it was something a father would do.

I treated my wife's daughters as though they were my own. The real father didn't have anything to do with them apart from asking for money. He had another family with children and seemed to not be bothered about his daughters. When I first met them they seemed happy to have a father - they kept asking me questions about the West and about sex. I think they realised that we in the West don't have a problem answering questions about sex (I suppose most of us don't - perhaps religious people would have a problem but they are mad anyway), unlike Thai people who are very prudish about sex. I know it sounds crazy with the ladyboys and men with boys and men with young girls etc but on TV, for instance, they blur out any nudity; guns and smoking. They also censor movies so sometimes movies don't make sense as they take out all the sex and violence - "Fifty Shades of Grey" didn't make a lot of sense when shown in Thailand! I was told that there is no sex education in Thai schools so there is a lot of ignorance. The stepdaughters were very interested in finding out about gay people; gay bars and gays in society in the West. Being gay in Thailand must be very difficult.

I also helped them in a practical and emotional way. They had a very difficult relationship with their mother as they lived with grandparents while their mother worked in the local city and when she was away for 2 years in the UK.

They would have a lot of arguments and the daughters would talk to me about the situation afterwards. I tried to listen and offer advice but above all else I supported my wife - that was a silly thing to do clearly! My wife did not approve of their lifestyle having girlfriends as opposed to boyfriends. My wife once told me that her father said that it was her (my wife's) fault that they were lesbians. My view when it comes to relationships is that you are attracted to who you are attracted to and it is not really anybody else business.

I began to get suspicious about what was going on before I found out what was happening with the loan. My wife had returned to Thailand for a visit in December 2016 and she had spent £2,000 while there. I obviously wanted to know how she managed to spend that amount of money in a week. At first, she tried to say she had lent money to friends and family which I could not believe. She eventually admitted that bills had not been paid in Thailand even though I had been sending money each money to Ploy (her daughter) to pay those bills as the daughter had used the money for partying. I call that theft! My wife disagreed but there were no proposals for repayment. I then started to ask questions about the loan repayment to me. Again was evasive. So I stated I wanted to see the bank account Ploy had said was open for me (remember she works for a bank). Eventually my wife admitted that Ploy had not opened the bank account and not made any payments with regard to the loan.

The arguments went back and forth and then I found out that the ex-husband was staying at my house. No one had told me about this or asked if it was OK. I asked can I go and stay in his house and can you imagine if I allowed my ex-wife to stay in the marital home? I decided at that point to make a surprise visit to my home in Thailand to find out what was going on.

I arrive unexpectedly and no one is there. Obviously, someone told Ploy as they arrived in her car and then left and never returned. My wife was not there as she was staying with friends and only returned after a week. Suggests they knew they had done wrong.

I returned to China and my wife then returned after a week to China. She began to say that she wanted to return to the UK as she was bored and fed up with China. I did not have a problem with that as I needed some space and time to think. My wife left at the end of February 2017.

A couple of months later I contacted lawyers in Thailand about the situation with Ploy. The lawyer I found in Bangkok wrote to Ploy and my wife was very angry. I had given them time to come up with proposals but they continued to lie about the repayments so the lawyer wrote to Ploy. This really pissed off my wife - not unsurprising but I did say to them that all I needed was an apology and what they were going to do to put it right. It was as though they were little kids who were found with their hands in the cookie jar but can't admit they have done anything wrong.

My wife said that Ploy's lawyer would deal with it and I thought why can't they just arrange to pay the money. I then received a phone call from my wife's best friend (Jane Doe - not her real name) - they had been friends for 14 years. They had worked together when my wife was working as a prostitute in London; they had stayed with each other; gone on holiday together and talked to each other for many years. She had stayed with me when my wife went back to Thailand and had come for dinner with me. We had also been away on holiday, together all 3 of us and the dog. She told me that my wife was telling stories about me that I wanted to have pictures of my step daughter's breast and other things. Unbelievable.

At that point I decided to divorce my wife - I can't stay married to someone I can't trust and who is telling malicious lies about me. I arranged to go to Thailand in July 2017 and went to my home in Chiang Mai to pick up my stuff and move it to an apartment where I had arranged in Bangkok to live with the girlfriend. Yes, I had a girlfriend and it had been going on for 4 years but was not that serious - it was more curiosity as the contacted me first, not me contacting her.

The girlfriend arranged the apartment and it was very nice. It was near Lotus/Tesco and the BTS (the BTS is the overhead train system in Bangkok which is a lot cheaper than the Underground in London). It was a big apartment - 3 bedrooms and 2 bathrooms on the ground floor and the swimming pool was a short walk away. I spent many a pleasant day sitting by the pool.

When I went up to the house in Chiang Mai the daughter did not come and see me - suggests someone was feeling guilty. She did, however, buy me food like bacon; sausage; eggs; bread etc. My wife made a point of telling me about this - even sending me a copy of the receipt. Perhaps she thought her daughter buying some bacon would make up for stealing money from me. They didn't know that I had gone there to pick up my stuff including the car and my motorbike. Clearly one of the neighbours told her as I received a text from my wife the evening the stuff went stating that she had told the police I had stolen my motorbike - my motorbike remember. A removal company was transporting everything down to Bangkok.

Next morning I arrive at the airport to fly to Bangkok and I receive a number of texts. One of the texts stated that we should sell the house and share the proceeds - which I agreed to. When I got back to Bangkok my lawyer wrote to my wife stating that I would agree to that with certain conditions which were to ensure that I received my investment back of 5m baht. I never received anything back so I instructed my lawyer to inform my wife that I was divorcing her.

My wife denies that this ever happened in the UK courts now - unfortunately for her I have the letter and other evidence that she knew I was divorcing her in Thailand. In August a month after the letter was sent to her about the divorce I started receiving messages from Mr. Mitesh (Mac) Varsani by email and then by using the Line app. His letter is in the Appendices. He basically was accusing me of bullying and being a paedophile. The interesting thing was that he stated that my wife had told him that I asked her to find a hitman to kill him for 5,000 baht (about £100). I know people are poor in Thailand but how could he believe that you could hire a hitman for £100. There are lots of stories of Westerners being killed in Thailand but the cost is many times 5,000 baht! A husband and wife were killed in Thailand but that cost 100,000 baht (about £2,000). He seems to believe this to this day. It shows how easy it is to manipulate some men.

Who was he? I met him through our interest in motorbikes and we went on a tour of Spain and Portugal together. During that tour he told me about his life. I don't know why but people always want to tell me about their life - I don't really want to know and I don't give a fuck about their life but they insist. Mac had had a bad life. He went to stay with his father in India or Pakistan and his father abandoned him. This was when Mac was a teenager. He had no money so he became a male prostitute. I can imagine that really fucks you up. Unfortunately, most of his clients were men aged over 50. So it was easy for him to believe that a man over 50 i.e me could be a pervert. Of course, he didn't need any evidence as my wife and her family could not provide any.

I was at an evening in Bangkok arranged by a group called Internations and I started to receive the messages. Internations is an international group that operates to bring ex-pats from all over the world together. I had ignored that email he had sent me in August thinking oh well he has vented off some steam and hopefully he will go away as I don't say anything. That clearly did not work. The messages were from then on all of the same theme - pervert; faggot; like to be fucked by ladyboys; Jimmy Saville; bully; perverted faggot and so on. The interesting thing was that he was talking about the marital assets by claiming that all the assets belonged to my wife and that she should have them all

- I could keep my motorbike and the small house but nothing else. It was interesting as that is what my wife offered me in discussions with her lawyer in Thailand about the divorce. Some of the messages are attached in the Appendices.

I did try to reason with him but he had clearly been worked on by my wife and her family with the same stories that my wife's best friend told me about. It was interesting later on that my wife tried to claim that she knew nothing about these messages even though I wad to discover on Ploy's Ipad that the first message I had received in August 2017 had also been sent to my wife. Also my wife had received copies of the messages from Mac as she showed them to her best friend Jane. Jane told me that my wife was very pleased about the messages - it was described to me that my wife had a smirk on her face.

I sent the messages to my wife who denied all knowledge of them. I even sent a message to my wife from mac where he states that I would have to change the marital bed as he had cum all over the bed and Ploy. He also stated that he was enjoying her tits knowing that I would never do so. I thought it was disgusting and also that I was not interested in my step daughter's tits bug clearly he had been told something different to that. My wife's reaction to this message was like a shrug of her shoulders and that Mac was her boss. I am astounded that a mother can think that it is alright for a man to talk about her daughter in that way.

I think at that point my wife was thinking I would react like a Thai man. Thai men do react in a shameful way if they are accused of such things even when they are innocent. It is used as a way of putting pressure to extract money. As everyone has said my wife did not know me after 12 years of marriage. I have said this many times you can accuse me of something or criticise me but if I don't value your opinion I don't care. What he was accusing me of - wanting sex with Ploy the stepdaughter - had been raised by other men over the years. They would say to me if I found her attractive and I always said the same that I didn't see her that way but as a daughter. I found it strange to be asked such a question as it never crossed my mind.

Ploy was working with Mac as he had come to Thailand to set up his solar energy company and I offered him help. My wife arranged a house for him to rent opposite us. I helped him with putting together his business plan as I am an accountant. Ploy helped him with translation and talking to Thai people. They developed a relationship but there was an early sign of the mental state of him. My wife passed on a message he had sent to Ploy about her dogs. I will be the first to admit that they were disgusting and unpleasant dogs as they were Shitzu (which was the correct name for them) but I would never attack them. In this message he admits that he attacked the dogs and hurt them - he didn't offer to pay the vet bills. Ploy was smitten with him and I saw a message to him from her to him talking about how she loves him but gets upset as he doesn't seem to acknowledge her.

After being told a tale by my wife and her daughter I am sure he saw himself as the knight in shining armour coming to the rescue of the damsel in distress. There were 2 other men who also got involved on that basis. One of them was Pete Griffiths in China.

Pete Griffiths was an interesting character. He was a teacher of English with me at the same company in China. We arrived at the same time but we were very different. He was, however, another one of those men who had allowed their wife on divorce to take everything from them and leave him with debts. He was very enthusiastic about everything to the point of being annoying. He also liked to be in control of everything and everyone. He had had troubled teens and had been in trouble with the Police. After that he changed his name. He said the reason he changed his name was that he did not want to be associated with his father anymore. However he worked for a local leisure centre in the UK and I know, as I worked for the Met Police, that your past is checked for any criminal activity. As he was working or having contact with children no convictions are spent i.e. no longer have to disclose to employers he would have been asked if he had changed his name. I don't think he did because when there was a burglary at the leisure centre the police found his old identity but it would have been on the leisure centre records when they were eliminating fingerprints. I don't think he was honest on his application or vetting form. I might be wrong but it does seem odd. He was involved in amateur dramatics in the UK and took a job teaching in Eastern Europe while he was on long term sickness absence from the leisure centre - so he got paid twice and received compensation for his sickness. I wonder if the leisure centre would be happy to know that he was claiming to be too ill to work yet was working in Eastern Europe.

I left the job in China without giving notice and that annoyed him. He even told the employers that I was leaving. I know this because they tried this stupid game with me asking for my passport on the pretext that the immigration wanted it - do I look that stupid? The reason that I didn't give them any notice is that Chinese employers of Westerners can be very unpleasant when you want to leave. The employers I worked for had screwed a teacher when they wanted to leave previously by withholding their last salary payment. So I collected my last payment and just left. They got a free week out of me as we were paid the 10th working day. Pete Griffiths was always happy about them trying to screw us over money. They would try the "we haven't been to the bank" excuse so I would say "I can't go to school today" and amazingly they would find the money. I never received any support from him about that.

He was enraged that I had left without telling the company in China. My view was what had it got to do with him. But it came down to him wanting to be the main man; to be loved and popular. I don't give a fuck about being popular - I will be nice and helpful and kind and generous and supportive but I don't give a fuck about your approval.

Where was I? I was suing my wife's daughter Ploy and I had told my wife I was divorcing. The messages started from Mr. Varsani (Mac). The messages have been relentless - going on for 2 years. Not only claiming I am a faggot; pervert; perverted faggot; a Jimmy Saville; but also that I would like being in prison in Thailand as I would be fucked up the arse! This went on for over 2 years. Can you imagine the possible effect on someone of such an outpouring of hate and obviously homophobic, It is only a short step to killing someone holding those attitudes. I have now reported him to the police in London it will be interesting to see if any action will be taken. It has been difficult to get them to investigate as their attitude at 1st was "he might not know it is harassment" Really! Anyway I am waiting to see what will happen with the police.

The messages I started receiving from him in August 2017 were continuing in June 2019!

I envy people like Mac Varsani because they are so ignorant and stupid. They will believe anything regardless of the facts or explanation Ignorant and stupid people like Mac Varsani have no doubt- do nto feel the need to check what they have been told with reality. It makes life very easy. For intelligent people the world is a complex place and intelligent people are always checking their perception of the world with reality and what they know about people's behaviour. It makes life complex. For stupid and ignorant people there is no uncertainty and doubt. Ignorant and stupid people can hold contradictory positions and be perfectly happy as they don't see the inconsistency. In some ways I feel jealous of such people like Mac Varsani. Unfortunately the UK has too many people like Mac Varsani!

Then in October 2017, my wife tried to claim the house from me by making a claim in the Chiang Mai court. I had a lawyer already so handed it over to her. The basis of my wife's claim was that she had paid for the house; I had not paid the lease premium and that she only gave me the lease out of love - so romantic. Later on, she was to say that I had forced her to sign the contract. She then stated that she gave me the lease to give me access to the house. How did I do that - hold a gun to her head; torture her! What nonsense it was.

A note about lease contracts in Thailand. It is not possible for a foreigner to directly purchase a house in Thailand. You have to protect your investment by either having a lease contract put in place for 30 years with a renewal for another 30 years or purchase the house through a company but the Thai national still has to own more than 50% of the shares. I, fortunately, contacted a lawyer when I was buying the house in Thailand in 2006 to protect my investment. She set up a lease contract and a loan contract. In the lease contract it stated that Mrs. Vale confirmed that the lease premium had been paid - so difficult to see how she could claim it had not been paid. However I paid a visit to the house and found all my original documents form 12 years before - I found the original bank statements showing the transfer of money and the original bank transfers. I could not believe that the daughter of my wife, Ploy, and her friend Mac (Mr. Varsani (had not checked all the drawers and cupboards to see if there was any useful information - that would be the first thing I would have done. The lawyer in Thailand was amazed that I had found the original documents and said to me I should buy a lottery ticket!

Mac was staying in my house even though I had sent him an email that he didn't have my permission to stay there. He kept claiming until February 2018 that he was not staying at the house at all. It was ridiculous as my neighbour was letting me when he was staying there and sent me photos of his car at my house.

The 2 of them - Mac and Ploy played various games. My lawyer had said that while the house was being sorted out that I give notice when I was going to the house - so I did. However one time they change the locks; another time they put an extra lock on the doors and another time they put a lock on the gate to the driveway. It was games being played. All the time they are denying that Mac is staying there. This went on for months.

I went up for the court case with friends abut the lease and when I arrived there were men installing cabling and cameras. As soon as I arrived they disappeared - they clearly knew I was the owner and I hadn't given them permission to install the cameras. They had actually installed cameras inside my house and one upstairs pointed at my bedroom. I traced the wire to the step daughter's bedroom and where there was a recording box connected to a computer. The room was locked so that I would have no access to it. I took out all the wiring and destroyed the cameras. I contacted my wife's lawyer and informed them that this was an invasion of privacy in my own home.

Mac decided to claim that he had paid for them and installed them as he was worried about Ploy's safety yet it had been agreed that Ploy would never be in my home when I was there. He also tried to claim they cost £2,000 (in Thailand!) and that he would sue me for the cost of them - I am still waiting! He also claimed in an email that as a tenant he had the right to change locks - really? So at first, he claims he is not going to my home and then claims he is a tenant - clearly not very bright!

I went one weekend to visit the house and every cup; glass; plate and cutlery had been used and discarded in the kitchen sink. I sent a message to them saying that they had left it in a disgusting state and Mac said that they hadn't left it that way - I thought he wasn't staying there! (That is sarcasm by the way)

I also lent a small amount of money to the youngest daughter Lek - it was about £500. She agreed to a repayment plan of £50 per month. Then she wrote to me saying she was going on holiday and could she postpone until after the holiday which was not a problem for me. Anyway she returns makes a few payments and then she just stops without any explanation. I attempted to contact her by Line app and by text and by email - no reply. I then tell her I am going to sue her and she states that she is going to pay me. Nothing arrives. So I sue her.

I then receive messages via Line from my wife supposedly which, I believe, was written by John Hatfield, who was her employer before we went to China in February 2016. The language used was too sophisticated talking about offshore pensions etc. There was one thing stated that I found amazing - he/she stated that when I supported Lek's application for a visa for the UK that I agreed to support her financially. I was not aware that I was expected to financially support her for the rest of her life. When did the UK government expect it to stop - when she is 40; 50; 60; 70 or no limit! It was such a ridiculous statement to make.

I had to sue her there was no other option. In her defence response she claimed that her family had paid off debts for me while I was in China so it meant she shouldn't have to pay the loan back. That was a ridiculous defence as no debts had been repaid as I checked on the credit agencies online. Before I left the UK I decided that I would max out my credit cards and get a loan and then leave the UK. Perfectly legal and the debts would be written off in 6 years. I could if I wanted to do go bankrupt - it would make no difference to raise credit as with the default on the credit cards and loan there was no chance of getting credit anyway. Going bankrupt would be advantageous to me on my return to the UK. Lending had got do strict in the UK that if you don't have 3 years of addresses and a history of credit you have no chance of getting a mortgage or credit card or loan. Practically no different from being bankrupt.

So both stepdaughters have borrowed money and are refusing to pay it back. My wife knew that they had borrowed money and that there was an agreement for it to be paid back so my view is that she told them not to pay it back and then lied to me about it. I wonder what sort of life lesson that teaches her daughters?

My wife now is suing me to claim the house from me in Thailand. Fortunately as I have said I had all the documentation for 12 years before. We went to court and my wife's lawyer asked me how I could prove I had paid the lease premium and I answered that it was in the contract my wife had signed confirming it was paid. The judge said that it was not up to me to comment on legal principles - I thought to myself I will continue to say it whether you like it or not. I didn't say that I just stayed silent.

The verdict was due about 3 months after the hearing - about February 2018. About a week before the judge's verdict was to be sent to us Ploy and Mac packed some of their stuff and left the house with the dogs - my neighbour informed me of this. It was obvious then that I had won as they had gone. No explanation was given and no messages from them.

Before that, after the court case regarding the house, I contacted a lawyer in the UK about a non-molestation order concerning my wife. I also contacted a lawyer about the messages from Mr. Varsani (Mac) - you know the ones that I kept receiving about being a faggot; perverted faggot; a jimmy saville; liking cocks in the arse etc - and a warning letter was sent to him. I knew that my wife was behind it as he had said that my wife had told him I tried to hire a hitman for about £100 in Thailand - really? He ignored the letter. I forwarded his messages to my wife and she kept saying that she was not involved. I eventually sent her an email showing how she and Mac were connected:

"If you come to the house Nicky has asked me to get rid of you. I will teach you a lesson" sent by email on 3 November 2017. "I might surprise you with a few guest waiting for your dirty pervert arse".

What pleasant person does this?

I have already stated that I find this sort of thing disgusting and beyond the pale but it appears that the UK and USA have become like it due to Trump and Farage and Brexit. I have seen over my lifetime that when I was young the UK was an intolerant society - adverts stating No Blacks; No Irish etc. And had become more tolerant with gay marriage; changing of laws on being openly gay in the Government employ etc but we seem to be going backwards. That is one of the main reasons I have left the UK - I see it getting worse in the UK as we leave the EU with no deal.

Mr. Varsani (or Mac) is a damaged person and obviously sees himself as the knight in shining Armour to save the poor defenceless woman from the rampaging Vikings or the from the Sheriff of Nottingham. It does not matter what they do or say, they are right about everything. He identifies so much with them that when he talks about the non-molestation order I had against my wife he claims that he was included as well. When he talks about himself he uses the "we" pronoun. He is so controlled that, even though he has lived in Thailand for 4 years that my wife and her family are using him. Thai people are very racist - they do not like anyone who is Black or Indian (that also includes Pakistan; Bangladesh; Sri Lanka etc. As soon as this is all finished they will drop him and not be interested anymore in him. They saw him as someone to attack me - an ally. Someone they thought could frighten me in some way. They just did not know. AS I have explained it is very very difficult to frighten or intimidate me. That does not mean that I am stupid but it is about assessing the risk and what potential they have to do you harm. My assessment of him as stupid and all mouth has proved to be correct.

It has been very easy to wind him up and when I do that he wants to prove he his a man by boasting about something. He has told me a lot of things - the latest one was that my wife had purchased a house in Thailand. I did not know that but now that I know I can claim 50% of the value on divorce. I warned my wife and her lawyer that the longer the process goes on the more I will find out.

From the very beginning in July 2017 I have offered my wife 50% of everything in Thailand but she came straight back with a demand for 80%. Then when she had worked out that it was up to me as to whether she got anything she then resorted to other tactics - stealing the assets and offering me a fraction of all the assets in Thailand to buy me out. I know the rules in Thailand in divorce and based on those rules I can claim all the assets.

I have been fortunate that throughout all the accusations made by my wife and her looking for allies to make statements in court about me they have refused to do so. My wife tried to get her best friend to make a statement against me - the best friend of my wife for 14 years - contacted me to let me know what was going on after my wife returned to the UK from China in March 2017. The housekeeper who had been in our employ for 7 years refused to make a false accusation of sexual harassment even though my wife offered her money and then threatened and the girlfriend of the youngest stepdaughter refused to give a statement against me even though she lived with us for 3 years. All the people that knew us intimately refused to lie about me. That is fortunate - can you imagine the position I would be in if they had agreed to lie about me?

The courts in Thailand have been fairer to me than in the UK. The police have been better to me than in the UK. Is that not a terrible indictment of the system in the UK as compared to Thailand? In Thailand everything is supposed to be corrupt; in Thailand the view is that no foreigner has a chance. This is not true as I have seen in my case - they have seen right through the antics of my wife and her family. When I go to court in Chiang Mai for yet another hearing (14 so far) they have chatted with me in their offices; they offer me tea and a seat to sit down while I am waiting. My wife's daughter Ploy has pissed them off because she was told that she had to come to court and she didn't turn up for mediation. This really pissed off the judge. It didn't help them that their lawyer was found to be lying and was told off by the judge!

A story was given out and was told to me by Mac that when I refused to pay bail in the criminal court that I was begging and crying - he even sent the message to me. I thought - really they believe that. Again it comes back to them having no idea about my character and how I will behave. I can understand Mac in a way - only in a small way. I tried to reason with him when he started sending messages accusing me of being a faggot; a Jimmy Saville; a pervert etc all because I am bisexual. For those who don't remember or know - Jimmy Saville was a TV star who was the public face of Stoke Mandeville Hospital in the UK that helped physically disabled people including children. Jimmy Saville used his power as a media start to sexually assault handicapped children. I can assure that I don't have any power to do anything like that and that I don't anyway.

In February 2018 we are in the position that I have won the case about the house in Chiang Mai so that is mine for the next 18 years and Ploy and Mac have left the house. All sorted. The non-molestation order I have in the UK has been revoked. The main reason for this is that my wife talks about finances for about 40% of her statement but I am not allowed by the judge to ask or challenge her about that part of her statement. I am also not allowed to challenge her witnesses about the lies in their statements. The judge also states that I shouldn't travel to Thailand if I am concerned about my safety at the hands of her family. A possible harasser has no limitations on their life while the victim should have restrictions placed on their life - a whole country, really! The non-molestation order is withdrawn.

2 weeks after that I am in Thailand. It has been agreed with my wife that she pick up all of her belongings on the 22 February. On the 21 February at 9pm at night she turns up in a gang of 8 to break into my home. I am standing on the balcony looking down on them and she is in the garden telling me she is going to break in. Then she does a bizarre thing - she starts to water the garden. There is my wife; her 2 daughters; Mac; 2 police officers; her lawyer and another man. Mac is urging me to come outside and I am thinking - do I look that stupid; the police officers are using their phones to video. Clearly, they want me outside to create a confrontation and then I get arrested - fuck that I thought. So I said to them the 1st person to break into my house will get hurt with this hammer! They then backed off. Mac keeps on taunting me and the neighbours phone the tourist police. At one point my wife tells me that her lawyer is there and I say

that I don't believe that he is a lawyer and the man wants to show me his Thai lawyer's club card!

Thailand has Tourist police. Their job is to deal with foreign tourists - deal with any disputes involving foreign tourists. Normally the disputes are over a bar girl saying she hasn't been paid or a tourist saying a bar girl has stolen his money.

After a stand-off one of the Police Officers comes to the door and asks if he can come in. I only allowed him in - as soon as I open the door my wife makes a rush for the door. I block her and push her back. Then the police officer tells her to back off. The police officer hands me the phone and I am talking to the tourist police. The police officer on the phone asked if I wanted my wife to leave and, of course, I said yes. So the phone is given to my wife and, knowing enough of the Thai language, I can understand that she is saying that she has just arrived from the UK; she has nowhere to stay; it is her home; she is talking to her husband etc. But he clearly told her to leave and they all went - the time was now about 11.30pm.

Let me tell you this - if anybody had broken into my home - they would have been hurt badly and the next mother-fucker too!

My wife had 2 police officers from the Thai police with her who were recording on their phones - interestingly the footage of the evening has never surfaced! It was quite clear that my wife was trying to goad me out of the house as her daughters kept calling me a pussy and Mac (the boy) kept saying come out for a cup of tea and a drink of whiskey. Shows how much he knows me as everyone who knows me knows that I cannot go anywhere near whiskey after a trip skiing to Italy when I was about 14 with my school.

As a digression. I went on a school trip when I was about 14 with my school to Italy on a skiing trip. At that time it was impossible to buy Johnnie Walker Red Label whiskey in the UK because of the regulations in the UK. I decided to buy a bottle for my Dad. 2 days before we are due to go back to the UK one of the teachers announces that we are not allowed to take any booze back with us to the UK. I have this bottle of whiskey - what to do? That night the 3 of us in the Chalet drank the whole bottle between us - I don't remember much of that night as I must have had a 1/3 of a bottle of whiskey. The next day I could not drink or eat anything - I just puked it back up again. We didn't get any sympathy from the teachers. This shows the difference between now and then (about 1976). Now I am sure that there would be an inquiry; parents would be summoned and discipline would be handed out to the teachers. Then the teachers gave us no sympathy and it was never mentioned again. Since then I cannot go anywhere near whiskey - just the smell of it makes me want to puke!

I had already arranged with my wife that she would pick up her belongings the next day but I think my wife had been drinking and had decided in her own mind that I was occupying her house. Being Thai she assumed that the police would support her but the police told her to leave. I think that is why she thought that turning up with a crowd outside my home would frighten me. Never happen.

In the meantime, I had started harassment proceedings against my wife in the UK. I talked to a lawyer about what was happening and was advised that I could get an injunction against her. I obtained an injunction in the UK as 2 days before the hearing my wife took secret photos of me which helped me to get the injunction.

As I was in the UK I had contacted my wife to meet to discuss what was going on. She agreed to meet. When I went to meet her she changed the venue suddenly to a pub. It was very crowded but she led me to a table. Unbeknownst to me, she had arranged for a friend or friends to be there as well to take secret photos of me. The meeting was a waste of time. I do not know why she sent the pictures after - was it to intimidate me? I don't know and I still don't know. But it did not help her as the judge granted the injunction on the basis of the pictures. This was 6 months before the house in Thailand was confirmed as mine in February 2018.

I was in the UK at the time at a non-molestation hearing against my wife. She had appealed the decision - I don't know why as you wait a year and it is revoked. But she did and I decided to go through the motions. I was more concerned about the house in Thailand as the decision about the lease was due that same week in Thailand. Naturally it went my way as the lawyer in Thailand who drew up the original paperwork did a good job. She did not get her costs as her lawyer did not submit the costs claim before the hearing.

I found out that I had won the case about the lease contract in Thailand. This meant that I had the house for the next 19 years to do what I want with. The lease is so wide-ranging that I can knock down the house if I want to. Even if the divorce went through in Thailand or the UK I would keep the house for at least 19 years. But as I had bought the house before we married the house is mine whatever happens in divorce as I kept all the paperwork.

I returned to Thailand to discover that my wife's family had taken out a criminal claim against me. My lawyer in Thailand was very worried but after talking to her about the maximum sentence I could get was 2 years in prison or being deported - that did not worry me. Everyone else was worried but me.

I returned to Chiang Mai to sort out the house and get it rented out so I could have the income from it. It was a tip. My wife's daughter Ploy and the man Mitesh Varsani had left rubbish everywhere. It took 20 bags of rubbish to sort it out. I packed up their stuff and informed them they could pick up their belongings. Remember ploy and Mac had left a week before the result confirming my ownership of the house.

It was arranged with my wife's lawyer that they would pick up their stuff. My wife wanted a key to the house - absolutely crazy. I would have probably been killed in my sleep by her or had my dick cut off. Thai wives do that a lot. Thai surgeons are now the world leaders in reattaching dicks. Thai women have been known to cook the cut off dick in a wok to make sure it can't be used again!

My wife unsurprisingly arrived the night before she was supposed to come. As I have said she came in a mob of 8. She turned up with her lawyer; Mac; her 2 daughters; 2 police officers (obviously family; and another man. The 2 police officers were filming - obviously hoping to use the footage against me. Strangely never seen again!

My wife had clearly been drinking and stated straight away she was going to break in. My reaction was quite straightforward - the 1st person to break in would get hit with a hammer. There is a standoff for 2 hours where her daughters are calling me a pussy for not coming out and Mac is calling me a faggot - quite clearly trying to make me angry to come out and then have me arrested. Eventually the police tell her to go home and they all leave.

It is then arranged that they would pick up their stuff on 28 February. They turn up late and I make sure I have someone listening in the UK in case they accuse me of anything. I discovered why they were late as my car had gone when I went to find it. I received an email from my wife stating that she had borrowed the car to go to Bangkok as she couldn't afford to rent a car as she had to pay for a hotel! That was a joke as she has a car but can't drive.

Chapter 12 I start to find out what is going on and has been going on

The car was taken along with my golf clubs; my international driving licence and the security access cards to the development. I sent them an email stating that I wanted my things back and the car. The only reply received was from Mac stating that he liked my golf gear!

From that day my wife has denied that there were any golf clubs in the car or anything else of mine. Is it likely that when you have a car that you don't keep anything in there? The golf clubs were there as I was visiting the local golf range to practice.

I then decided to find out what had happened to the houses I had invested in not far from the main house on a separate development. I had been informed by my lawyer that my wife had taken out a loan against one of the houses for 600,000 baht (about £16,000) while we were in China. This was 6 months after we left for China. Clearly, my wife had decided to get hold of my money! She claimed that she borrowed it to help a family member - trust me my wife would not do that for a family member!

I then found out that my wife had sold the houses. She had sold one of them about 5 years before (that I have not confirmed at the Land Office - though I will). She had sold the 2nd property in 2018 for 1.6m baht paying off the 600,

000 baht loan. I will be suing her for that. The reason I question what happened to one of the houses is that she never mentions it in any statement in the UK or Thailand. She might still have it or I was paying the mortgage on it and did not know it and then she sold it. I will be checking the land office when I next go back to Thailand.

I met with a new lawyer in Chiang Mai who found out that the car had been sold. I had changed lawyers as the criminal claims were coming thick and fast from my wife's family. There were suing for anything - mainly defamation. Silly things like I raised a question on Facebook about her daughter not asking me if I would look after the daughter's dogs - really defamation!. I also said to Mac if you are calling me a pervert when I have done nothing then what about my wife's brother who actually went to prison for raping an 8 year old girl. It turns out that Mac knew this and that was OK with him. Wow, an interesting moral compass! Anyway, I was sued for defamation for one email to one person about it.

In the end, I said in court that I was not going to pay bail and then I sent a letter to the court that I was not going to bother anymore after 13 claims and that they should decide what they were going to do - put me in prison or stop these claims. Remember it is estimated that there are approx 60,000 people in prison in Thailand for not paying bail. So don't think they don't send people to prison in Thailand for not paying bail.

My next move was to take my wife to court in the UK for harassment and theft - after all she has sold a car I bought; stole money from a joint account; stole houses and my things. Also she has been inciting people to attack me.

Chapter 13 UK courts and Thailand courts

It has been amazing the different approach taken by the UK and Thai courts. You would think that the Thai court would be corrupt and automatically support my wife as she is Thai. You would assume that the UK court would base its decision on the evidence and not prejudice. It has been interesting.

My wife has made the most outlandish claims and allegations. Provided no evidence to support those claims and yet the court has accepted them in the UK. I have provided a veritable orgy of evidence and this has been ignored. In fact, in the harassment case, the court stated that they would ignore the evidence regarding my wife's claims concerning the financial part of her statement. The financial claims in her statement constituted nearly 60% of her statement. I was not allowed to question her witnesses - who had lied as well which I will come on to later.

I was even told by the judge that if I thought that my wife would take action against me in Thailand then I should not go to Thailand. Wow, so as a potential victim I should avoid a whole country!

The Thai courts have realised what is going on as they have seen so many claims by Thai wives trying to claim falsely assets in a marriage.

Chapter 14 Tax evasion and lies by her so-called witnesses

This has dragged on so long with my wife refusing to negotiate and even after 18 months of negotiation in Thailand turning around in the UK and stating that there was no divorce going on in Thailand means that this saga will continue for another 2 years.

What this has meant is I have had a chance to do what I do best - that is to find out information about someone on the Internet and from records held by the UK government and credit reference agencies. As a consequence, this information will have big consequences for my wife and possibly for her lawyer.

I have discovered that my wife has been evading tax from the very 1st time she came to the UK in 2004. She was here originally on a fake passport and a visa she bought at the British Embassy in Bangkok. The embassy is well known in Thailand for the ease that a Thai person can buy a visa to the

UK through an agent. The agents are so confident of getting a visa to the UK that they advertise a guaranteed visa or your money back. That is what my wife did in 2004. However, she didn't have the money so she borrowed it from the criminal gang in Bangkok. The amount she borrowed for the visa was £25,000.

I know this as her friend she was working with informed me of this and many Thai women working with my wife had parties to celebrate paying back the money.

They earned the money by being prostitutes in the UK. I met my wife when she was a prostitute. So as you can see big money for the British Embassy employees in Thailand.

I have no idea if my wife paid it back but she was successful as a prostitute. She was very popular. The idea was suggested by her aunt but the suggestion originally came from her mother when my wife was about 17. People in the villages in Thailand see that prostitutes earn money to buy land and property so they encourage their daughters sometimes to become a prostitute as well because they see the money. My wife comes from a very poor background in a small town in the mountains surrounding Chiang Mai. In Thai culture, the pressure is on the daughter to support her parents while the son does not have to. Of course the brother is a waste of space as he went to prison for raping an 8 year old girl. This something my wife claimed did not happen under oath when giving evidence in the non-molestation appeal in the UK. The brother also gets financial help from my wife. The time in prison has been confirmed by a Mr. Griffiths and Mac (the man).

So I was able to get into my wife's tax records held by HMRC and what I found was most illuminating. I discovered that the address she claimed to have been living at for 2 years was not her actual address. This meant that one of her witnesses had lied (Vantanee Gresophon) in her statement when she claimed that my wife had been living with her for 2 years and therefore had witnessed some events between myself and my wife. This could not have happened if my wife was not living there. I found out my wife had been living at 4 Popes Lane, Ealing and not 23 Longley Avenue as she claimed and others claimed.

In sworn statements in the UK in cases **E66YJ959; E68YM375; F02CL161; F52YJ639; ZW17FO0001; and** BV18D34525 Mrs. Vale has made a number of financial claims that show that she has been involved in tax evasion on a large scale and could possible owe over £150,000 in unpaid tax over a 15 year period - this does not take into account the penalties that could be imposed.

This also involves the companies she works for facilitating the tax evasion by deliberately providing false information about employee's pay to the HMRC in the end of year returns.

Mrs. Vale has also been aided and betted in her tax evasion by the employers she has worked. Across the Thai massage business, there are various tax evasion schemes being operated. These usually involve a low amount of pay being showed in the Contract of Employment but the actual amount is higher which is made up in a cash payment OR the employer just pays them cash and there is no contract. The pay in the contract is set at just below or at the tax-free threshold for Income Tax in the UK so as to appear legitimate to HMRC. One of these systems or a mixture has been used by all the employers of Mrs. Vale in the Thai massage businesses she has been involved in. The employers have openly been facilitating tax evasion

I know this as I was an accountant for all of my career. I also talked to the owners of the business and also the employees when I picked up my wife from her place of employment.

The tax evasion helped the companies as it was difficult to recruit into the Thai massage business and it helped the companies as their declared costs in accounts were lower than actual costs. This helped the companies to show profits in order to raise money for expansion from the banks. They were excluded from year-end audits as they would incorporate each branch as a separate company. A year-end audit would have shown that the costs were under-declared in the accounts by the simple audit test of the sources and uses of funds statement that reconciles the Profit and loss with the balance sheet. The massage business also gains as the under declaration of Employees Income leads to lower Employers National Insurance costs.

The UK Treasury loses both direct tax (Income Tax and National Insurance) and also Employers National Insurance contributions.

The Thai massage company will issue a fixed monthly pay contract - if they issue a contract at all. However the employees are always paid on the same basis. The basis is a commission-based system - the employees are guaranteed £10 0r £20 per day but the employees have to do 2 massages and then they get paid a commission rate for each massage after the 1st 2 massages.

The employers do not normally provide paid holidays; sick pay; comply with minimum wage legislation and routinely ignore the working hours legislation. Mrs. Vale has stated in her sworn statements that she regularly worked 60 hour weeks and 6 days a week

Mrs. Vale has made the following financial claims in the sworn statements in all the cases mentioned. She has been supported in these claims by notably her employer Mr. John Hatfield of Sansara Massage Limited.

Mrs. Vale has been employed since at least 2010 - however her tax record at HMRC shows only employment from 2013. She also claims that she was employed from 2004 to 2006 - however there is no record of this employment at HMRC and, in fact, she had no National Insurance number. From 2004 to 2006 she was in the UK illegally and worked as a prostitute - she was arrested in a brothel in Worthing in 2006 and then deported.

Mrs. Vale acquired a National Insurance number in 2007 when we returned to the UK after our marriage. You need a National Insurance number to work in the UK and to be able to claim free health care and benefits.

The estimated tax evaded from 2004 to 2019 is as follows based on her statements as she can only have had this income in the UK as she had no income in Thailand:

Assets Purchased	Value (£)
House in Thailand	86,000
2nd House in Thailand	15,000
Car	16,000
House built in Thailand	20,000
Household expenses paid in Thailand (£500 per month	60,000

from 2007 to 2017)	
Household expenses paid in the UK (approx £800 per month in 2015)	10,000
Financial support to family in Thailand (£400 per month 2004 to 2019)	72,000
Living expenses in the UK - travel; food etc (2004 to 2019 £500 per month)	90,000
Rent 2004-2006 (£200 per month)	5,000
Rent 2017 to 2019 (£700 per month)	17,000
Savings in Thailand after return to Thailand from the UK	25,000
Buying illegal visa in Thailand	25,000
Total estimated wealth accumulated from 2004 to 2019 (approx)	**445,000**

Mrs. Vale is also claiming to live at 2 addresses in the UK - 23 Longley Avenue, Wembley and 4 Popes Lane, Ealing W5.

Mrs. Vale can only have earned that money is the UK as she has no income in Thailand. In the period 2004 to 2019 Mrs. Vale has only declared approx £35,000. A total possible under declaration of approx £410,000. This does not take into account additional monies for flights and birthday presents and clothes purchased in that period.

I understand that the tax calculation would be based on this year's tax rates as it would be declared this year. This gives a total tax evasion by Mrs. Vale of approx. £165,000 plus approx £12,000 National Insurance - a total of £177,000. Plus potential penalties of 100% to 200%. Mrs. Vale can pay the tax and penalties as she has recently sold some assets she claims to have purchased over the period 2004 to 2019.

If this is multiplied across all the potential employees in the Thai massage industry in the UK this is clearly a major loss of tax revenue plus the loss in Employees and Employers National Insurance revenue.

Her lawyer Staines and Campbell of Ealing W5 must be aware of this tax evasion as I have informed them of it and I am certain they have not reported it to HMRC as they are required by statute. How many other clients do they have that they know are involved in tax evasion or have unaccounted for wealth?

I have all the sworn statements made by Mrs. Vale and can provide them and I am willing to give evidence as I have intimate knowledge of Mrs. Vale's employment history; pay; working conditions and claims. I can also provide documentary evidence as to the value of the assets claimed to have been purchased by Mrs. Vale over the period 2004 to 2019. Mrs. Vale's best friend can also attest to the fact that Mrs. Vale was working illegally in the UK from 2004 to 2006 and that she was deported, as Mrs. Vale's friend worked with her at the time. I am sure that you will be able to gather evidence from her lawyer Staines and Campbell.

One of the companies (Nuad Thai) that Mrs. Vale worked for in Northwood and Ealing was involved in, what can only be called, major tax fraud and trafficking. The method they employed is that they charged the women from Thailand £25,000 for the UK visa and promised them accommodation. The accommodation was not forthcoming and they were forced to live in the massage shop without any heating in all weathers including the British winter - which can be very cold. The women then worked off the debt of £25,000. Naturally the company did not pay tax on the charge of £25,000 and they were not audited as each shop they opened was incorporated as a separate company. They were helped by their accountants who knew what was going on and aided and abetted the scheme.

Thai people see the UK as a corrupt and an easy touch as the experience that they have had with the British Embassy in

Bangkok, Thailand was that if you have the money to pay an Embassy worker you were guaranteed a visa to the UK with minimal checks. This was well known in Thailand - all the way from Bangkok to Chiang Mai (700KM from Bangkok).

Mrs. Vale has also committed an offence under section 40 of the British Nationality Act 1981 on grounds of fraud, false representation or concealment of a material fact or on grounds of conduciveness to the public good when she concealed that she had been deported for being in the UK illegally when she applied for British citizenship.

In the film, V for Vendetta on of the detectives states that the best place to go for factually correct records is the tax authorities as everyone has a vested interest in making sure they are accurate - the Government so it collects all the tax due and the taxpayer as they don't want to pay too much tax. Also what people don't realise is that when you tell your employer a change of address the employer when preparing payroll is asked if they want to update the tax department - why would any employer refuse?

Also in the UK, every employee receives a P60 which is a record of pay and employment for the tax year but at the same time the record is sent to the tax authorities with your new address. Naturally HMRC update their records. I

I discovered that my wife had not had a national insurance number from 2004 to 2006 when she was here illegally. She claims that she was - however any employer who offers you a job for you to get your work visa in the UK would have to also register you as an employee and that would generate a National Insurance number. You keep the same number in the UK regardless of your change of circumstances - for instance changing your name on marriage. The 1st time my wife had a National Insurance number is when I applied for one for her in 2007 after we got married. So no National Insurance number from 2004 to 2006 and no record of any income.

My wife claims that she worked for most of our marriage from about 2010. However, there is no record of any income until the 2013-14 tax year. So another 3 years missing. From 2013-14 there is a record of income but it is not complete as she works up to September 2015 but no record in the tax year 2015-16. Then we leave in February 2016 to China.

On her return from China in March 2017 Mr. Hatfield in his sworn statement claims that my wife worked for him at Sansara Massage in Ruislip in 2017. However again no record of any income at HMRC.

My wife then starts work for another massage place Serena Health and Beauty in Bond Street earning £1,000 per month - this just happens to be just below the threshold for payment of Income Tax in the UK.

A note about how the Thai massage business in the UK operates with regard to payment of staff. Staff do not receive a fixed amount each month (even though the employers claim that this is how staff are paid). My wife has worked for a number of massage companies in London and each has operated in the same way. The staff are paid a minimum of £10 to £20 per day and they start to earn commission on each massage after they have completed 2 or 3 massages with no commission. My wife was very popular so earnt a lot but the employer only reported the same amount each month - at or just above the tax threshold. Doing this made it unlikely that HMRC would investigate. The staff would be tax, paid in cash and not pay tax. This would also help the employer as they would report lower costs and hence bigger profits which would help in raising finance form the banks for expansion or overdraft negotiations. It would not be caught as they would register each shop as a separate business and therefore stay below the audit exemption. If they were audited any accountant would pick up the discrepancy between costs and cash.

All the companies my wife worked for operated in this way. My wife knew that she was evading tax as she was the manager of a store in a large company in Thailand and was responsible for payroll. She knows that she is evading tax.

The other problem my wife has that she has unaccounted for wealth as a result of her claims in her sworn statements. She has claimed that she paid for the houses in Thailand - a total of £115,000 plus the car (she claims 50% of that) £16,500 plus savings of £8,500 plus coming to the UK in 2004 to 2006 plus ongoing expenses each month of at least £1,000 each month since 2004. A total of since 2004 of about £480,000 - yet when she was working she was only earning £1,000 per month. That could be a potential tax bill for tax evasion of £120,000 plus penalties of 100% to 200% - a potential total of £240,000 to £360,000. her lawyer Staines and Campbell could have problems as lawyers have a statutory duty in the UK to report tax evasion by their clients - I have informed her lawyer of this information. I wonder if they have reported the tax evasion?

I warned her lawyer that if I was given time I would do what I am good at - finding information.

It helps that when I was in my 30s I was a hacker - I could hack into anything. I gave that up as it was boring - too easy. Also with my skills as an auditor, I know where to look for things that don't make sense and where to check if figures in different places support each other.

It will be interesting to see if HMRC will do anything with regard to the Thai massage industry or my wife and her blatant tax evasion which is supported by her own sworn statements and that of her so-called witnesses.

I am issuing legal proceedings against my wife and her so-called "witnesses" in the UK for perjury.

Chapter 15 Met Police and courts reaction to the harassment

It has been interesting that the courts have seen you through the lies of my wife and her family yet the UK courts have not. In fact, the UK courts have accepted the lies of my wife; her family and silly men and not allowed me to challenge them. Not allowed to question them in court and not allowed to question my wife about her claims.

My wife has presented no evidence to support her claims about assets in the marriage. I have not been allowed to question her claims in her sworn statements and even when I have provided evidence that she is lying in sworn statements in the UK that has not been allowed to be put to Mrs. Vale.

My wife gave a statement to the court that was over 50% about the financial side of our marriage. However I was told by the judge I was not allowed to question her about financial claims. This has been the case throughout the claims in the UK. Any evidence I give is ignored and any claims my wife makes are supported however crazy they are and the paperwork shows it. The evidence is overwhelming. One judge said to me that I should avoid Thailand – the whole country and yet still revoked my non-molestation order against my wife.

10 days after the non-molestation order is revoked in the UK my wife arrives at my home in Thailand in a group of 8 and tells me she is going to break in. Shows her attitude and behaviour.

I complained to the Metropolitan Police in the UK about the messages; threats and behaviour of Mitesh (Mac) Varsani. You know the over 100 pages of messages; texts and emails telling me that I was a faggot; a perverted faggot; a Jimmy Saville and many other things. It was all centred on my sexuality. He even said that I should go to prison as I would like it up the arse!. It was amazing his attitude when you consider that my wife's brother (Ampol Tharaso) had been sent to prison in Thailand for raping an 8 year old girl and he knew about this as he informed me that my wife's daughter Ploy Laowanit had confirmed this to him. That was OK it seems but someone who had never been involved in anything like that deserved to be attacked and threatened because a pretty woman involved in a divorce told him a few lies.

I have stated in an earlier chapter that I am bisexual but I am not sure that I am. I don't like sex with men but I like sex with women and ladyboys. I like sex with ladyboys because they look very sexy and gorgeous. Any man who sees a picture of ladyboys or sees them thinks that ladyboys are very sexy. There are some men who say that they would never have sex with ladyboys however we all know that the most venomous of deniers are usually involved in such practices. We have many examples from the UK politicians who passed draconian anti-gay laws but then were involved in gay parties. And also we have the example of priests in the Catholic Church who would denounce child abuse but would then go into the vestry and have a young boy suck their cock!

I met one of those in China. Pete Griffiths who I worked with in China was a man who quoted the right-wing Christians in the USA – it is exit only when they denounce gay sex. I do not believe men who say that as I am sure that they have at some point had anal sex with a woman and enjoyed it. It is the hypocrisy that I can't stand. Pete Griffiths liked to portray himself as someone who cared; who loved you and wanted to present himself as an alright guy. You know the type – he loves everyone but he wants to be in control. If you don't do what he wants you to do he will stab you in the back. We have met them all. He had a very strange relationship with his daughter. I always find it odd when a man calls his daughter "princess". This suggests something weird about their relationship particularly when that daughter is in her 20's!

Mr. Varsani is a coward there is no doubt. He comes in a group of people to threaten me and he runs away when he sees me when he is on his own! Now, most civilised societies have rules about homophobic behaviour – they usually call it hate crime and it is a criminal and civil offence.

I contacted the police in March 2019 about the messages and the threats including the clear threat to "sort me out" if I went to my home in Thailand. You would think with over 100 pages of the same homophobic hate over a period of 2 years being sent that the police in the UK would spring into action. That did not happen. That is not unusual as the police in a recent report were criticised for their lack of support for the LGBTQ community in the UK. The reaction is one I should not have been surprised by (I should say their lack of action) based on my experience in the Metropolitan Police in London.

Remember I was 12 years in the Metropolitan Police in the central accounting function and as a Trade Union representative. As a result of those roles I had access to all areas and spoke to people in all aspects of the Metropolitan Police. Also because of my experience and my ability to understand systems I soon saw what was happening in the Metropolitan Police.

The Metropolitan Police is a quasi militaristic organisation where to be rewarded you have to do as you are told; not question what goes on and to accept all the traditions and systems of the organisation however bad they are. It does not matter how good you are at your job what counts is doing it the organisation way without question however badly the organisation behaves and however much it breaks the law. There is no room for principle in the Metropolitan Police in London. It is a tribe and if you accept the standards; the ethics and the attitude of that tribe you will be rewarded – however low those ethics. I saw it many times.

Managers did not have ethics – those who did, left or were forced to leave. Police officers could steal from the organisation and it would be excused as a failure of the system or that the rules did not cover the situation so it was a failure of the organisation. In any other organisation it would be called stealing and the employees would be fired.

A couple of very good examples of the behaviour of people in the Metropolitan Police are the following. There are many.

The scandal of the American Express card. This was big news and there were lots of meetings about the issue in the Metropolitan Police. For those of you who don't know what this was about. Police officers were given an American Express card to pay for expenses when on an investigation. The process was very clear – each month the credit card bill would be sent to the Police Officer and they had to indicate which charges were personal expenses. The local accountants in each borough were supposed to police this and ensure that the returns were made on time. Now if Police officers did not make the return then after a certain amount of time the Metropolitan Police was supposed to just charge all of the credit card charges to the Police Officer. I think you can guess what happened – a lot of Police Officers just didn't bother and the local accountants were too frightened or had gone native – you don't question a Police Officer, he is your superior! It came out that Police Officers used the card to buy sex toys; pay for hotel rooms for their mistresses and buy computer equipment for their own homes. It totalled many thousands of pounds.

The Metropolitan Police basically wrote off the money owed. As an accountant and Trade Union official I did ask the question – why wasn't the money deducted from their pay at the time? The response was that it might have caused hardship. I never saw the same attitude taken when Police Staff (administration staff) were overpaid pay due to a mistake by the Metropolitan Police! No Police Officer faced charges for theft. It was theft they knew the rules – any other organisation would have at least fired them and recovered the money.

Another example was the case of the Sergeant who had an affair with the PCSO (Police Community Support Officer). I was involved in this one for about 18 months. I loved this one as it gave me a chance to show up the behaviour of Police Officers. A Police officer was having an affair with a PCSO. She ended the affair with him. Unfortunately he didn't like that. So he started a campaign of harassment against her. He would damage her bicycle at the station and thought up ridiculous allegations. Eventually she had a breakdown – she gave her socks to a tramp when she was on duty in Oxford Street and also drove her motorbike into the sea. She was detained under the Mental Health Act in the UK. I guessed that the Police Officer had used a Metropolitan Police car to visit her for sex while he was supposed to to be on duty – the other officers knew this was going on but protected him and helped him in his campaign. He also had allegations from the public about his behaviour. In the end, the Metropolitan Police caved in and gave her money and a clean record in her employment even though she had been off sick for 18 months. It would have been very bad newspaper headlines as the Borough Commander then wanted to dismiss her even though it was obvious that the staff member was covered by the Equalities Act because of her disability.

Another story was the story of the gay man in the Met Police who was harassed by Police officers to the point that he couldn't face meetings about his situation. In that meeting he would crawl under a table and start to cry as he was so badly traumatised by the treatment he received. This was a man that had had a successful career in Banking before joining the Metropolitan Police. He was intelligent and had been working in the City where you cannot say that people are liberal in their attitudes. Again no action was taken against the Police Officers who undertook a campaign of harassment against a member of Police Staff. This was a typical pattern. A member of Police Staff who was considered guilty of the slightest indiscretion such as having a county court judgement debt was fired while a Police Officer used police resources to impress his mistress by using a Metropolitan Police American Express card to ensure that rose petals were strewn over the bed at an expensive hotel and had no intention of paying it back. Talk about double standards.

If the Metropolitan Police wanted to get rid of you then they would use any tactic. Human Resources in one case I had even en told the manager involved to change their view of the allegation – the manager took the view that the allegation was a minor infraction but Human Resources told him to change his recommendation to state that it was a gross misconduct issue. Unfortunately the Met Police being incompetent gave both papers to me for the hearing. One was signed and one wasn't – interestingly the manager signed the original recommendation but didn't sign the HR view. The Met Police handled that case so badly that they had no option but to come to the conclusion that the Police Staff member could not be fired. She did have quite a long holiday – she was off for 6 months fully paid as the Met Police could not get its act together. The issue was quite minor as it involved some drunkenness in New Year's Eve and an argument about a restaurant bill.

Amazing the reaction of the Met Police when the police officers have committed many illegal and immoral acts which have gone unpunished. That is the real problem with the Met Police that Police Officers are protected no matter what they do. It is endemic from the very top to the bottom. It will not change until someone outside the Police Service is given the power to sort it out and put in place a culture that does not reward subservience to the power of a police officer and instead gives power to staff to stop behaviour that is clearly not acceptable

I was a thorn in the side of the Met Police. This was shown by how negotiations would change when I came in to support the Union member. A perfect example of this is a negotiation I became involved in after the negotiations had stalled for 6 months. This involved a number of issues but again involved Police Officers being Neanderthals with regard to racism. I think I still hold the records for the biggest settlement without going to court. I had been told by the Union lawyer that the maximum the Union member could expect to get in court was about 50% of what I negotiated.

There were many stories like this in the Metropolitan Police. You have to understand that even in the 1980s the Metropolitan Police sacked gay men if they admitted they were gay. Senior police officers I encountered were racist and sexist and homophobic. It was rife and I would assume it still is as the reforms instituted and then continued by Ian Blair were then quietly dropped when Bernard Hogan-Howe became Commissioner of the Metropolitan Police. Police officers were very happy when that happened and Police Staff were very disappointed. Police Officers felt that they were going back to the old regime where they could do anything (even if it was illegal) and be protected by the organisation. I have many details about the dinosaur attitudes of the Metropolitan Police. Many strange events would not be tolerated in a normal organisation. This is because loyalty is rewarded more than skills.

I should therefore not have been surprised by the attitude of the Metropolitan Police to my allegation of harassment as they see me as a faggot. I have given the Metropolitan Police over 100 pages of evidence and yet they keep asking for more. At first they said to me that they would visit Mr. Varsani to inform him that his behaviour was unacceptable – this did not happen. Then they said they would take my statement and they then said that Mr. Varsani might not know it is harassment (can I use that excuse if I am caught speeding!). I pointed out the Police Officer looking into this (PC Louise Behenna 3482WA

Response Team B (Ealing), Metropolitan Police Service, West Area (WA)

Ealing Police Station - 67-69 Uxbridge Road - W5 5SJ) that the law and the case in the Supreme Court in the UK meant that the defendant did not need to know it was harassment, the test was that of a reasonable person. Also there are limited defences for an allegation of harassment. Obviously this was clearly a hate crime. How much evidence do you need for the Metropolitan Police to arrest someone for a hate crime and for harassment? You must note that there are only 2 acts for it to be considered harassment.

The Police Office was stonewalling me and coming up with excuses for Mr. Varsani's behaviour from the beginning. No wonder the LGBTQ community needs to take it's own actions when the police are not prepared to support the community in London from homophobic violent men. It is clear from the 100's of pages of messages from Mr. Varsani that he is prepared to go "queer bashing" as it used to be called in the "good old days" when faggots knew their place! I think that Mr. Varsani will be visited as he did me in a group of 8 people! It will be interesting to see how the Metropolitan Police reacts if Mr. Varsani receives the same treatment as he did me.

Chapter 16 What now

At the moment I owe about £20,000 in legal costs to my wife awarded by the courts in the UK. However as you probably guess I have a plan for that as well.

My wife's daughter Ploy has stopped paying the 7,000 baht she was ordered to pay by the court to pay in Thailand so I will be taking her back to court to claim her assets.

It has not been decided as to where the divorce is going to be - in the UK or Thailand. I contested the jurisdiction of the court when I received papers in the UK. That will take time as there are have been so many cuts in the Public Sector in the UK that to get replies and action in the Family Court will take months.

So the next stage is to claim the car back and the houses sold in Thailand. This will be done in the UK. The judge has put a stay of 6 months on the car claim as my wife's lawyers said that it should be part of the divorce negotiations so I asked for a time limit as they are not interested in negotiation but only in theft up to date. My wife's lawyers have made it clear in an email that my wife is not interested in negotiation.

A note about my wife's lawyers Staines and Campbell in Ealing, West London. They know that my wife must have been involved in tax evasion as my wife has claimed in statements that she has acquired a large number of assets in our marriage and that she paid for them even though is hardly any record of income and paying tax in the UK. I have sent them the evidence. Lawyers have a legal duty to inform HMRC (Her Majesty's Revenue and Customs – UK Government tax department). It would be interesting to know if the lawyers have done so.

The big question is - should I have been nice in Thailand and offered 50% of the assets from the start? I don't think I should have done so. What do you think?

My wife has finally got me in prison in Thailand - only for a week. The next stage is a hearing about the jurisdiction of the

UK in the divorce. I think I will win that. I have not heard from my wife's lawyers for 6 weeks - I don't think she has paid them as her legal bills in the UK must have been at least £20,000. My wife hoped I woudl pay them but I sorted that out legally in the UK by going bankrupt. Mr Varsani finally got me and broke both my arms.

I am winning and if the divorce is in Thailand then I will get all my money back.

In the next book I will be describing my time in prison and how I had the support of the gay crowd in the prison.

How am I winning? By being very strong emotionally; having paperwork and not giving in or being frightened by bully boy tactics of my Thai wife. I have received lots of threats and been lied about but you need to be strong.

Appendices

Mitesh (Mac) Varsani

Hates gay men (or faggots as he calls them) – watch out if you work with him and know him

Ampol Tharaso (Mrs. Vale's brother)

Raped a girl aged 8 years old -works in a shopping mall as a security guard in Thailand. The shopping mall knows that he is a child rapist. He probably enjoys his job with all those young girls at the mall!

Ploy Laowanit who claimed that I took her to brothels for 3somes in Thailand. Why then did she still stay with me when she has her own flat when I came to Thailand? Lied about paying back a loan to me and stole from me

She works as an Investment Advisor for Bangkok Bank in Chiang Mai. The bank knows she has defaulted on a loan and lied in court and stole from me

John Hatfield – the owner of Sansara Massage Limited in Ruislip, West London who perjured himself in statements and facilitates tax evasion by employees in the UK. Perjured himself in sworn statements

Vissannee Laowanit (Lek) who stole £250 from me which was a loan and then lied in sworn statements in the UK and Thailand

Pete Griffiths – who pretends to like gay men but always uses the terms used by right-wing Christians in the USA (exit only). He also lied to his employer was on long term sick leave and was actually teaching in the Czech Republic and changed his name to avoid his criminal past. He gained from these lies as he received money for his so-called ill health. He was found out by the police when there was a break-in at the leisure centre where he worked. It means, of course, that he must have lied on his vetting form when he applied for employment with the local Government employer. Like all homophobic men, he loves lesbian porn

Finally my wife. Of course I didn't know that she had started stealing from me already. She has shown contempt for the legal system by lying in every statement to the courts in the UK and Thailand. I also didn't know she had a boyfriend who is about 75 years old (so I have been told) – why type of women go out with old men 20 years older???

Some of Mac Varsani messages - do you want to work with this

man!

So will I... with your big fat face..

I'll make a brochure in thai n English n post it on FB...

Because itsss you... I'll even do a Facebook paid Ad n promote it. Lol.

"Look out for the English pervet"

"Hide your daughter's " 😊 😊 😊

21:34

Im indian for sure.. but we are better human beings than you are or can ever be.

Am i stingy? Not as you. But i will do everything i can to do the same, as what you doing to these 3 girls.

Enjoy life without anyone caring for you when you old in 4-5yrs lol..

All the young whores you with.. they will give u good time, n suck you dry, shag younger side lover on your expenses nwhen your broke.

They will leave you. Like everyone in your shitty life 😊 😊 😊.

You know what ploy told me last year before all this shit you started...

She said... if anything happens to nicky, i will take care of john for all his life. N you went and done all this drama n threatening n you spoilt it all. Not for her... but for yourself

21:42

What i say to her. Is good riddance of that dirty old pervet fagot.

You dont deserve good people in your life. I hope these whores of yours does the same shit you doing to your current family, X family.

21:44

No reply. Just reading 😊 😊 😊
22:35

So funny if u think u can get ing arrested 😊 😊

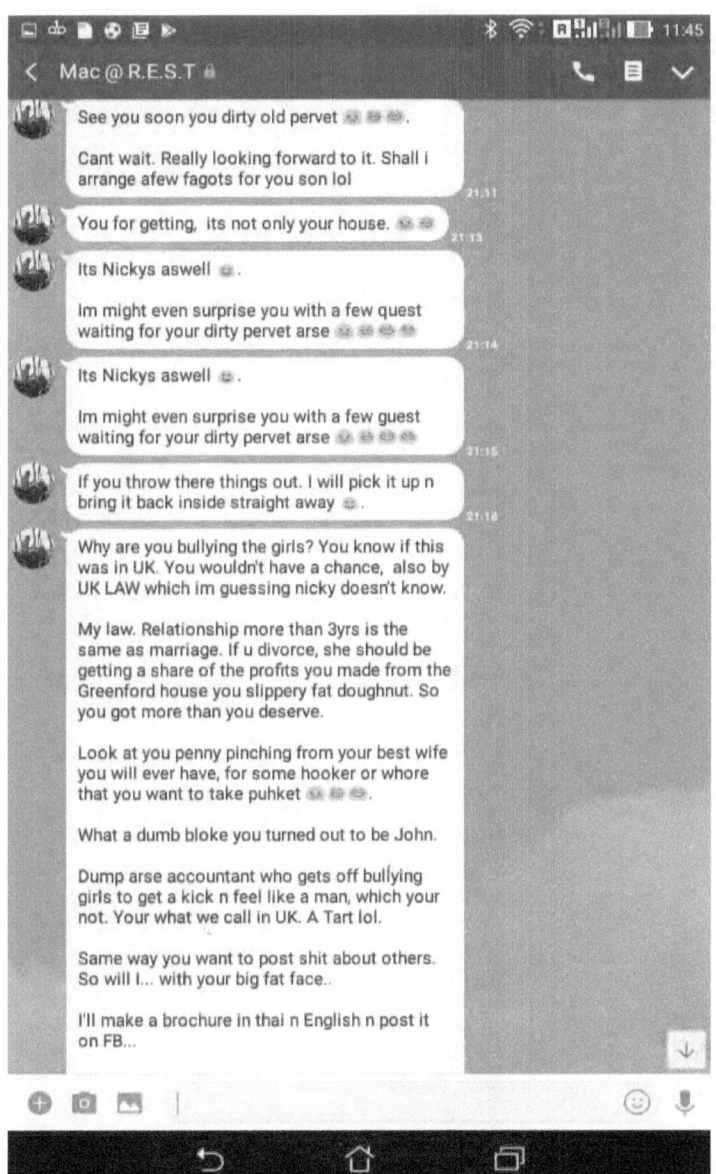

See you soon you dirty old pervet 😠 😠 😠.

Cant wait. Really looking forward to it. Shall i arrange afew fagots for you son lol
21:11

You for getting, its not only your house. 😠 😠
21:13

Its Nickys aswell 😐.

Im might even surprise you with a few quest waiting for your dirty pervet arse 😠 😠 😠 😠
21:14

Its Nickys aswell 😐.

Im might even surprise you with a few guest waiting for your dirty pervet arse 😠 😠 😠 😠
21:15

If you throw there things out. I will pick it up n bring it back inside straight away 😐.
21:16

Why are you bullying the girls? You know if this was in UK. You wouldn't have a chance, also by UK LAW which im guessing nicky doesn't know.

My law. Relationship more than 3yrs is the same as marriage. If u divorce, she should be getting a share of the profits you made from the Greenford house you slippery fat doughnut. So you got more than you deserve.

Look at you penny pinching from your best wife you will ever have, for some hooker or whore that you want to take puhket 😠 😠 😠.

What a dumb bloke you turned out to be John.

Dump arse accountant who gets off bullying girls to get a kick n feel like a man, which your not. Your what we call in UK. A Tart lol.

Same way you want to post shit about others. So will I... with your big fat face..

I'll make a brochure in thai n English n post it on FB...

Honestly you the 1 who messed up nicks life by telling her lets retire, i will takecare of you..

Once you realised its not cheap to retire n made poor nickys life a living hell u fat doughnut. What kind of husband gives his wife 100 baht to buy dinner, you worser than indians 😶. All the brain, but no heart. You are like a child who doesnt get his way n makes others life a nightmare.   your proper childish,

Why act all proud , big man n show off retiring n dragging nicky. Asking her to leave UK , n travel with you, for you to mess it all up..

For an accountant, who should know his numbers before making a life changing offer to nicky n making her retire with you to baby sit you your stupid arse, your sure are 1 of the dumbest accountant i know 😶 😶 😶.

And now your acting like a typical english nob head who's moaning n begging for money for 3 hard working girls .

You are so sad n pathetic John boy. No wonder your 1st wife left you n now nicky dont want you. Nicky was the best women you will ever find John.

Honestly, me n nicky didn't see eye to eye regular, cause we both strong characters with our strong opinion. But to be honest, i have so much fucking respect for her than i do for you, she's independent, raised the girls until she met your miserable face, n she does what she says. ... even after all this headache you causing her, she a million times better than you John.

We where mates once apon a time. N you didn't have many n dont have many.. i mean friends who care about you like we did. You will never have them if u behave like this in life.

21:10

Tue, 5 Sep 2017

Hey Johnnn.

The Biggest pervet in chiang mai, who wants to see his step daughters boob job, you filthy disgusting man...

By the way.. excellent tits which you wont see you pervet 😠.

Beautiful boobs 😠.

Hows shagging lady boys going? Its still a bloke end of the day. 😠 😠 😠. So now adays you shagging blokes i see lol...

Honestly you the 1 who messed up nicks life by telling her lets retire, i will takecare of you..

Once you realised its not cheap to retire n made poor nickys life a living hell u fat doughnut. What kind of husband gives his wife 100 baht to buy dinner, you worser than indians 😠. All the brain, but no heart. You are like a child who doesnt get his way n makes others life a nightmare. your proper childish,

Why act all proud , big man n show off retiring n dragging nicky. Asking her to leave UK , n travel with you, for you to mess it all up..

For an accountant, who should know his numbers before making a life changing offer to nicky n making her retire with you to baby sit you your stupid arse, your sure are 1 of the dumbest accountant i know 😠 😠 😠.

And now your acting like a typical english nob head who's moaning n begging for money for 3 hard working girls .

You are so sad n pathetic John boy. No wonder your 1st wife left you n now nicky dont want you. Nicky was the best women you will ever

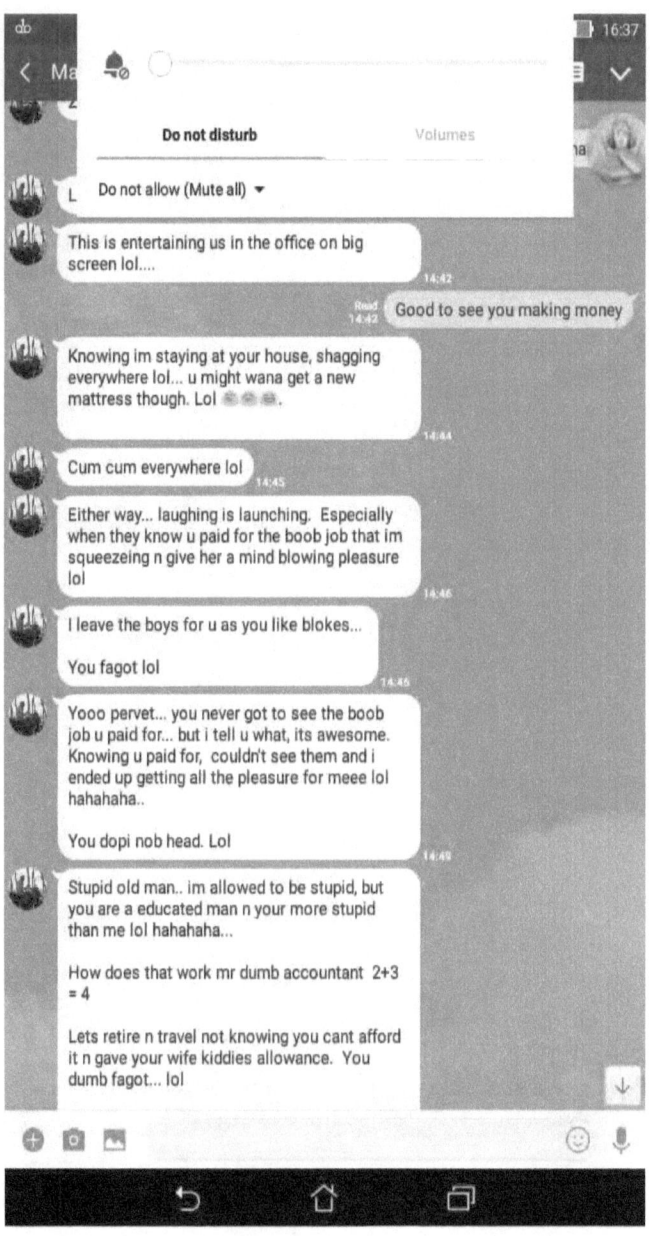

16:37

< Ma   ☰ ⌄

Do not disturb   Volumes

Do not allow (Mute all) ▼

This is entertaining us in the office on big
screen lol....

14:42

Read
14:42   Good to see you making money

Knowing im staying at your house, shagging
everywhere lol... u might wana get a new
mattress though. Lol 😄😄😄.

14:44

Cum cum everywhere lol
14:45

Either way... laughing is launching. Especially
when they know u paid for the boob job that im
squeezeing n give her a mind blowing pleasure
lol

14:46

I leave the boys for u as you like blokes...

You fagot lol
14:45

Yooo pervet... you never got to see the boob
job u paid for... but i tell u what, its awesome.
Knowing u paid for, couldn't see them and i
ended up getting all the pleasure for meee lol
hahahaha..

You dopi nob head. Lol
14:49

Stupid old man.. im allowed to be stupid, but
you are a educated man n your more stupid
than me lol hahahaha...

How does that work mr dumb accountant 2+3
= 4

Lets retire n travel not knowing you cant afford
it n gave your wife kiddies allowance. You
dumb fagot... lol

⊕ 📷 🖼   ☺ 🎤

Page 350

www.ingramcontent.com/pod-product-compliance
Lightning Source LLC
Chambersburg PA
CBHW030607220526
45463CB00004B/1195